THE
FASTEST GUN IN HOLLOYWOOD:
THE LIFE STORY OF PETER BROWN

**By Peter Brown
As Told to
Alexx Stuart**

Wild Horse Press
www.WildHorsePress.com

Dedication

This book is dedicated to my wife Kerstin, who is my love and inspiration; my children, their spouses and my grandchildren whom I love more than words can say; and to the memory of my parents, Mina and Bud, who passed on their dedication to hard work; and especially to my mom's love of the arts.

Peter Brown

ISBN-10: 1940130018
ISBN-13: 978-1-940130-01-9

Published By Wild Horse Press
An Imprint of Wild Horse Media Group
P.O. Box 331779
Fort Worth, Texas 76163
1-817-344-7036
www.WildHorsePress.com
ALL RIGHTS RESERVED
1 2 3 4 5 6 7 8 9

Special Thanks

A very special thank you to Alexx Stuart and Diedre Kaye without whom we would not have this book! Also to my family, especially my brother Phil, who jogged my memory more than once about our childhood; to Wyatt Mc-Crea for jumping in on short notice to write the forward and his lovely wife Lisa for being such a great friend to my sweetheart; to my best friend Rex Hardin and his wife Robin for always being there for us; to our friends CJ and Bob for their support; to our friend Rodney for never getting tired listening to my stories; to my business partner Greg Long; to my Fan Club for always coming to all the events and supporting me; and, of course, to Robert Fuller and his beautiful wife Jennifer . . . we go back a long time.

Here's to many more years!

Peter Brown

Table of Contents

Foreword
by Wyatt McCrea

I first met Peter Brown at one of the annual Lone Pine Film Festival gatherings in Lone Pine, California, where we were both invited participants. We were staying at the same motel. On the first evening, I walked out of my room on my way to one of the festival events when I spotted Peter sitting in a chair under a tree reading a script and enjoying the late afternoon air. I had never really been properly introduced to him, so I decided to just go over and say, "Howdy!" From the moment we shook hands, there was a sense of instant kinship — that rare kind that makes you feel like you are in the presence of a family member rather than somebody you just met. As the sun set over the Sierra Mountains, we chatted casually about the script he was reading, about "the business," and about my grandfather and uncle. There was just an easy feeling about that meeting; it was as if we had known each other for many years.

Well, from that moment on we became great friends. We have ridden in the Rose Parade together, been frequent guests in each other's home, become business partners, and attend many of the same film festivals. We even enjoy a bit of Mexican (or Italian) food together whenever the opportunity arises.

My wife Lisa and I had the proud privilege of being guests at Peter's marriage to his wonderful wife Kerstin (or "KK" as we call her). The way they met and the fact that it led to matrimony is a wonderful story of the unknown journeys life can take. Peter couldn't have asked for a better partner; I know they've been a real blessing for one and other. Also, I think he finally met his match!

Always the consummate professional, Peter has forever been grateful for his long and storied time in front of the camera entertaining millions of viewers. His career would be the envy of most actors. From forming a theatre troupe while serving in the army to his chance encounter with Jack Warner, Peter's career has spanned over fifty incredible years! He has gone from spending many hours in the saddle on great television westerns to the steamy story lines of daytime drama to the silver screen starring as a surf idol and a battle tested soldier, just to name a few. Peter has been one of the busiest actors in Hollywood! He is always true to the characters he portrays and has provided us with countless hours of wonderful television and film entertainment. His is truly a lasting legacy!

After all these years of being "in the business," having known and worked with many of the biggest names in the industry, Peter has now taken the time to share some of those incredible experiences with you on the pages that follow. I know you'll be intrigued and captivated as you explore the life and times of Mr. Peter Brown. His story is a fascinating journey!

I am honored beyond words that he asked me to share this foreword with you. I am proud to be able to call him "mi amigo" — my friend!

"Son, I'm the only one left."
— Jack Warner, when asked by me if he was one of
the Warner brothers

Chapter 1
The Westerns

There's a Hollywood legend about Lana Turner and how, as a 16-year old student at Hollywood High School, she skipped a typing class and ended up at Schwab's Drug Store on Sunset Boulevard. Turner was sipping a Coke when she was spied by the publisher of *The Hollywood Reporter*. He was enthralled by her beauty, and before she knew it, "The Sweater Girl" was in the movies.

My story begins much like Lana's; we were both discovered on Sunset Boulevard, only instead of goofing off at a drug store, I was spotted at a gas station . . . sort of. And I was not "the girl in the sweater"; I was "the grease monkey in the coveralls."

I had been out of the army about three months when I took a job pumping gas at a Union 76 station. I had come to Los Angeles to pursue my dream of a career in show business, but the bills still had to be paid.

At the time, I was doing *Desire Under the Elms* at the Horseshoe Stage Theater. When I say "doing," I actually mean I was stage managing the show and understudying the lead while performing a small, very small role in Act III. I definitely needed a second job; thus, the gas station.

So there I was pumping gas one day when fate came knocking on the door. It's funny: if I had been in the back working on a car or hitting the head and one of the other guys took the next car to come in, my career would have been completely different. Just shows you how life can turn on a dime.

I was at the cash register inside the station when a giant, black Cadillac drove over the signal hose letting me know we had another customer. I bounded out in my usual happy manner.

"Fill 'er up?" I asked the elderly, cigar-chomping, unhappy-looking gentleman in the car.

"Yeah," he harumphed, paying me no never mind. Undeterred, I pressed on.

"How's your oil?"

No response. I began cleaning the windshield as I kept up my sales pitch.

"How about those tires? Want me to check the air?"

Still no response. I flipped open the hood and checked the oil, water, the whole nine-yards. I noticed his fan belt looked a little worn.

"Well, how about if I —"

"Hey . . . kid!" he exclaimed. "Just fill the damn tank!"

He turned away and went back to reading his copy of *Variety*. Cigar smoke belched out the window.

Suitably chastised, I zipped my lip, closed the hood, and topped off his tank. He held out his "charge-a-plate" (what we called "credit cards" in those prehistoric days) as he continued to read. Now, normally I didn't pay much attention to the name on the cards, but for some reason when I ran it, I noticed it read "Jack L. Warner."

JACK L. WARNER!

My mind raced off in a million directions. I quickly hustled back to his car.

"Excuse me, sir, but are you . . . are you one of the Warner Brothers?"

He put down his paper and unclenched his teeth from around his soggy, black cigar. Ever so slowly, a knowing smile made its way across his face.

"Son," he said, "I'm the only one left."

This was it! This was my big opportunity. I had a rehearsed spiel touting my background and talents that I often practiced, not that I ever thought I'd have a time to use it. But this was it . . . this was my big chance.

Since I was holding his charge-a-plate, he couldn't leave until I gave it back to him. So dangling it in front of him like a carrot, I speed-talked about my experiences from New York to high school to Alaska to L.A. I was so nervous I hardly knew what I was saying, but I'm pretty sure I even invited him to my show at the Horseshoe Stage Theater. I ended my screed with the statement that being in movies was my lifelong dream. I stood back and then waited for the inevitable rejection.

I guess it amused him because he hadn't cut me off. He eyed me up and down like a butcher checking out a side of beef.

"That's nice for you kid," he said after a long pause. "Good luck."

And like that, he signed the receipt, coughed up what sounded like a giant ball of phlegm, and then drove off. I futilely waved, both at him and the exhaust smoke. I figured that was the end of it. And it was . . . at least until the next day.

I was in the station bright and early the following morning when the phone rang. A gruff voice began barking out questions on the other end.

"Yeah, can I speak to, uh, uh, . . . let me speak to Peter Brown."

"This is Peter Brown."

"Yeah? Well, this is Solly Baiano. I'm the head of casting and new talent for Warner Brothers."

My heart skipped a beat.

"Yeah, so the thing is, I don't know who you know, kid, 'cause it don't normally work like this, but I have orders from the top to bring you in a for a screen test."

I was stunned. For the first time in my life, I couldn't get my mouth to work.

"Kid? Kid, are you there?"

I nodded vigorously.

"Yes, yes, I'm here, Mr. Baiano," I managed to sputter out. "So . . . what's next?"

"Like I said, kid, you come in here for a screen test. That's 'what's next.'"

And in the big picture, what was "next" was the beginning of my lifelong career in show business.

Solly had me do two screen tests. The first stage was a personality test. They had me sit in a chair facing six people and a camera and answer their questions. It was a little intimidating but nothing I couldn't handle.

I guess I passed that test, because they then gave me a scene to learn. They paired me up with another aspiring actor testing for a contract and we performed a scene on camera. The actor they had me working with was Ralph Vitti, now better known as "Michael Dante."

Michael was a fine actor. I lost track of him for awhile, but we eventually worked together a few times. We really got to know each other at celebrity tennis tournaments to which we were both invited. He was, of course, a fine tennis player . . . still is. He now lives in Palm Springs where he has his own radio show. Michael remains a good friend to this day.

We both must have impressed the Warner brass, because shortly thereafter, Michael and I each signed seven-year contracts. I was beside myself with excitement. The contract guaranteed me pay for forty weeks a year, working or not; my salary was to be $125/week for the first six months. After that, I got a $25/week bump.

You'll probably find it hard to believe but I took a pay-cut to work at Warner's; I was actually making more money at the gas station. But that certainly didn't matter to me. I was happy to get to do what I wanted. I was in show business and nothing could stop me now. With this contract, I knew I could be a star.

Warner Brothers supplied everything for us actors: classes, drama coaches, everything. They even arranged dates for us, "dates" being a loosely used term for getting their young actors and actresses publicity.

My first such date was with Connie Stevens. We went to a premiere where we walked the red carpet. It was a baptism by fire, of sorts. The photographers, using those old, giant flash cameras, shot away as if they were fending off Taliban attackers in an Afghanistan ambush. I can't remember the name of the movie, but you can bet your bottom dollar it was made by Warner Brothers.

The studio wanted its actors' faces on-screen so that viewers would get to know you. They wasted no time with me. My first job for the studio was a guest appearance on *Colt 45*. Wade Preston was the star. He was such a nice man, but it seemed to me his heart really wasn't in the show or in acting. Sure enough, several years later he gave up show biz to become a private pilot in Europe.

I began showing up on many of the other Warner Brothers' westerns, making multiple appearances on some of them: *Maverick*, *Sugarfoot*, and *Cheyenne*. I met Clint Walker on the *Cheyenne* set. He was a mountain of a man, but a gentle giant. He gave me probably the most important bit of advice I would ever receive, at least for my time acting as a cowboy.

"Peter," he said, "if you're going to do westerns, you cannot count on the studio to supply you with your basic needs. They'll always be looking at the bottom line and you'll end up with crap! The three things any self-respecting cowboy actor must have and that you'll need to get on your own are your hat, your gun, and most important of all, your horse."

Those were words I would always remember. They would be incredibly helpful to me in the upcoming decade.

I made it to my second year with the studio but was still waiting for that one, big break that would put me on my way to the top. I remember that it was a Saturday morning. I was renting a little place in the Hollywood-Burbank area in a housing development called the Hollywood Knolls. It was situated high up above the Warner Brothers' studios. I was living in the basement of the house, although it was on ground level. I had a kitchen, bathroom, and one large room. Utilities were included in the rent. What more could a young, aspiring actor like me want?

To give my pad a sense of a bedroom, I built a frame and then covered it with burlap in order to divide the large room into two smaller rooms. I was so comfortable and just really enjoyed living there.

Anyway, I was out front having my coffee, just soaking in my basement-view when the phone rang.

"Hey! Brown! It's Orr!"

William T. Orr was Jack Warner's son-in-law. He was also executive-producing a new western that some of us had heard talk about on the studio back lot. It was tentatively called *Lawman*.

"Morning, Bill."

"I have to ask you a question," he said. "Do you know how to use a 45?"

"Certainly, Bill," I responded. "You just put the record on the record player spindle and push 'Play.'"

"No, you idiot! A pistol! A 45 pistol"

"I can learn," I said, then paused to catch my breath.

This could be just what I'm waiting for I thought.

"Then learn . . . fast!"

"What's this all about?" I asked.

"*Lawman*! My show! You must have heard. It's the story of an old time sheriff . . . and his deputy. Jules Schermer is producing it. Peter, I'm telling you, Schermer wants you! He had his pick of all our contract players and he picked you! He said he wants Peter Brown for the deputy on *Lawman*! You're going to be Deputy Johnny McKay!"

"Bill, if you're kidding me I swear I'll — "

"Peter, I'm serious. Be at Schermer's office 9 a.m. Monday morning!"

Jules Schermer? I thought. *That name sounds familiar.*

Then it hit me. In early 1958, Jules Schermer had produced a movie called *Onionhead* starring Andy Griffith. In it, I played a sailor sitting at a bar. The role was small, so small in fact that my part ended up on the cutting-room floor. Even though my name appears in the credits, my face never made it into the movie.

Nevertheless, I had a good work ethic, "no small roles" and all that. In my entire career, I never missed a call time. If I was supposed to be on the set at 8 a.m., I'd show up at 7:30 a.m.

One morning when I was there ahead of everyone else as usual, I was in costume and sitting at the set bar. That's when Jules noticed me. He came over and started a conversation. It began with why I was there so early, but soon moved into a discussion of horses and all things western. It was a short, and what I thought insignificant, conversation, but now, months later, it was most unexpectedly paying off.

I wandered outside and looked down at the studio lot. It was indeed a wonderful day. And it was only going to get better. After all, they were now going to be paying me to pretend I was a cowboy.

Remembering the words of Clint Walker, I immediately called Arvo Ojala. On western sets, Arvo was known as "The Gun Wizard." I needed his help in finding me a gun, and then I wanted him to teach me the fastest of "fast draws."

Arvo took me shopping for a gun we would both like. After a short search, we found the perfect weapon . . . or I should say "weapons." We came up with a matching pair of six-shooters, their serial numbers in sequence so we knew they were made at the same time. What I really liked about them was their pearl handles. Their grips were so smooth; they would just glide into and out of my hands.

Arvo and I took the guns to an ace gunsmith and holster maker, the renowned "King of the Fast Draw" Andy Anderson. He would be able to modify the guns to my specifications. Andy examined them both in and out of my hand. He then cut down the trigger guards, making them lighter, and trimmed the hammers so that my thumb would come off them much faster. He also smoothed the cross-hatching on the hammers so that my thumb wouldn't drag on them, allowing it to slide off quickly. It may not sound like much, but Andy made those guns extremely easy to shoot. When he finished, he handed them back to me and then said one simple word:

"Practice!"

And boy, did I ever. At first I kept dropping my gun, so often that I was afraid I would wreck my new, finely tuned weapon. As a cure for my ham-handedness, I stood on my bed while I practiced and let the mattress cushion absorb my quick-draw mistakes. It took a while, but then one day it all fell into place.

Once I became proficient and comfortable on the draw, I began practicing flipping and twirling the gun. It wasn't long before I could flip it and have it land perfectly in the holster. It may sound weird, but I practiced so much with my gun that we virtually became one.

I was now fast . . . very fast! A magazine had set up a contest to see who was the fastest gun in Hollywood; they used an electric timer to determine drawing speed, quite a big deal back in those days. There was a plunger on the clock-timer that would release when you started your draw. The firing of your gun would stop the clock.

This contest drew many of the western stars of the day eager to "slap leather"; they were a very competitive bunch. But amazingly enough, the young buck from the new *Lawman* show took first place. I was just so at ease and confident with that gun.

Regarding the title of "Fastest Gun in Hollywood," that was just one contest. I'm sure there are other actors who would dispute my claim to being the fastest. I just know I've never been beaten in any one of these types of contests. And there is also this: in his wonderful book, *The Fastest Guns Alive: The Story of Western Fast Draw*, author Bob Arganbright quotes Andy Anderson, after being asked who the fastest of the Hollywood fast guns was, as saying, "If Steve McQueen, Ben Cooper, Peter Brown, Nick Adams, and Steve Benson were shooting it out for points . . . it would be one hell of a shoot out. Those guys are good! Real-Damn-Good!"

Even today, I get remarks from people, mostly at western shows, about how comfortable I seemed to be with my gun. They made similar comments about me and my horse. All I can tell them is, "I was in heaven."

Speaking of horses, securing one was my next "must have." If I had left it up to Warner Brothers, I would have been riding a different horse every show, just getting the next horse in line from the company stables. Working with the same horse is so important: you get to know his likes and dislikes, and he gets to know yours. It's kind of like a marriage: the two of you need to act as one, be a team, and you can't do that if you're with a different horse (or woman) each week.

One of my buddies, J.J. Smith, was a trainer of jumping horses. J.J. was a great guy. He worked at the Silver Lining Stables owned by the late Jerome Kern's family. Kern was an American composer of musical theatre and popular music. You may remember the song Kern wrote in 1919, *Look for the Silver Lining*, made more popular years later as a theme song for the International Ladies' Garment Workers' Union.

I alerted J.J. to my situation. He went to a claiming race in Tijuana, Mexico, and soon after, I received a phone call.

"Brown!" he yelled into the phone. "I've got your horse! You're going to love him! He looks great, he can jump, and boy is he smart!"

Ever the practical man, I blurted out the first thing that came to mind.

"How much?"

"Uh, . . . he's under . . . a thousand," J.J. stammered, now not quite as enthusiastic.

"How much under?" I asked.

"$750."

"Bring him in," I said.

And J.J. was right. I did love that horse.

I was able to repay J.J. the favor during the 70's when I was shooting a *Streets of San Francisco* episode. J.J. was at the Cow Palace in San Francisco for a national competition. He had three horses there, so he needed help exercising them. So every day for a week, I would ride *Jingle Jangle*, the number two ranked jumper in the world, trotting him around the arena and practicing jumps. *Jingle Jangle* was a great horse, and it was a real honor just to be allowed to ride him.

"*Amigo*" was the name of the horse J.J. found for me; he was the horse I would use throughout my years on *Lawman* and *Laredo*, although I soon developed another name for him through no fault of my own. I was in my kitchen looking out the window on the third day of our new rider-horse partnership when I realized *Amigo* was wandering loose in the yard. I knew I had secured his stall door the night before, but somehow that rascal had figured out how to work the latch. I started to head out to take him back, but I stopped when I realized he was definitely heading somewhere. To my utter amazement, he went right to the tack room, which was where we kept the horse feed. He then proceeded to open that door and began to eat his fill.

I just stood there, mouth agape.

When *Amigo* was done stuffing himself, he carefully backed out of the tack room, nosed the door shut, and then went back to his stall. My backyard horse-feeding operation had now become "self-serve."

"Oh, he's not as smart as he thinks he is," I said to myself. "He forgot to latch the tack room door."

It became readily apparent to me that this guy needed a new name, so I gave him one:

Houdini!

I named him after "Harry" Houdini, the great magician and escape artist of the early 20th century. Harry didn't have anything on my horse when it came to escape tricks.

The least difficult of the three items I had to have on any good cowboy show was my hat. I didn't want it to look like everybody else's, so I got one that was tipped down in front. That allowed me to utilize a nice acting effect where I would look up from under the brim when confronting another character. It became a trademark move of mine.

Lawman debuted on October 5, 1958, which just happened to be my twenty-third birthday. I jumped in with both feet, giving it my all, and before long it was a hit. I was soon being recognized on the street. To my delight, the money got substantially better. Thanks to the quality of the show, I felt I'd have a good job for a quite a while. It was now time for me to stretch my wings.

I was in the Green Room, the studio restaurant at Warner's, when I overheard two actors talking about a little house for rent in Burbank; the address was 1521 Morningside Drive. So, I decided to take a trip to Burbank to do a walk-through. It turned out that the house was large enough for three people, but what really intrigued me was that out back there were two horse stalls. Being as it was so close to Warners, I could ride *Houdini* to work. That really appealed to me. The wheels began spinning.

I had overheard that Robert Colbert was looking for a place to live. He was a cowboy actor like me, so I pitched him on the possibility of becoming roommates. He loved the idea, especially the part about the horse stalls since he, too, owned a horse. Once in the house, I rode *Houdini* to work every day, keeping him in the Warners' horse barn when he wasn't needed on the set.

Times were good at the Morningside house. We had one huge party that attained almost mythic status. We had a pretty good sized fountain just outside the front door. We drained the water out of it, lined it with plastic, and then filled it with liquor. At that moment, all bets were off.

My buddy Robert Fuller had a few. He soon began to enjoy himself perhaps more than he should have. He found a giant glass bowl full of matches. Emptying the bowl, he took it outside and dipped it in the fountain, the fountain full of liquor. Once filled, he then took the giant glass out back and set it down in the stall of *Houdini*, my horse, my livelihood. It got ugly very fast.

Houdini didn't seem to mind the offering at his feet. In fact, he rather appreciated the service and immediately took to the glass. He guzzled the amber concoction like he had been doing it all his life. And I, proving to be no more intelligent than my horse, then tried to ride him. A stumbling horse and a drunk cowboy were not a good combination.

I fell off immediately.

Looking back all these many years later, I can readily see what a stupid move that was. I blame it all on the exuberance of youth . . . and on Robert Fuller.

I was only twenty-two when we started filming *Lawman*, and I still had much to learn. The major force behind my education in television was the star of the show, John Russell, one of the nicest men I've ever met. He was soon to become my co-star, mentor, teacher, but most of all, my friend.

Already cast in the role as the "*Lawman*" before I came aboard, John was 6'4" with perfect posture, a former Marine with the most intimidating, steely gaze on television. He was the perfect hire to be the courageous, no-nonsense Marshal Dan Troop. He once told me that he modeled Troop after a superior in the Marine Corps, a man in his mid-forties. True to his calling and bucking the industry's infatuation with youth, Russell added gray to his hair in order to play the character a decade older than he himself was.

My introduction to John Russell occurred at a little drug store across the street from Warner Brothers. Bill Orr told me that that's where John wanted to meet with me. I was apprehensive at first

(L-R) John Russell and Peter Brown on the set of *Lawman*.

about talking with this very tough-appearing, more experienced actor who as the star of the show, had every opportunity to have "diva-like" tendencies. My worries were quickly put to rest.

John Russell was a true gentleman, the consummate professional actor. Our lunch meeting was most cordial. As we ate and talked, I remember thinking, *Now this guy looks like a marshal.*

Our relationship stayed pretty much the same over our four years together. We never had an argument. John was always thinking how to make the show better, causing me to do the same. He stayed in great physical condition, a regular workout-aholic. Along with his piercing gaze, his sharp voice let everyone know you need to respect this man.

John taught me so much about television and motion picture acting. "Focus on the camera," he'd always say. "Use your eyes to tell the story, not always your mouth. That's where your focus should be. Your eyes are your tool."

John did movies right up until three years before his death in 1991. I especially loved seeing him with Clint Eastwood in 1985 in Eastwood's *Pale Rider*. More than twenty years since *Lawman*, John still looked the part of a steely-eyed, no-nonsense marshal.

I think John and I had a classic mentor/protégé arrangement in *Lawman*. Some people have described it more as a father-son relationship. If you've seen any promos for the series, we were usually described as "the lawman of strength and purpose and the boy he trained to fight by his side." That described the two of us pretty well.

It took a lot of determination on our part to maintain the integrity of the show and characters while dealing with a parade of ever-changing writers and directors, a bare-bones budget, and what can only be described as frantic shooting schedules. After all, we were doing one to two shows per week, thirty-nine episodes per year. Speed and quality were two variables that were often at odds with each other.

Lawman cast (L-R) Peter Brown as deputy Johnny McKay and John Russell as Dan Troop.

Early on, John and I could see that it would be up to us, as a united front, to protect the quality of *Lawman*. I dedicated myself to all things western, honing my gun handling and riding skills while paying strict attention to John and his suggestions about my acting. The two of us worked hard to make *Lawman* the highly-rated show it was. We had to. We weren't getting a lot of help from the studio.

Warner Brothers was not known for extravagant spending on its television productions. All their shows were filmed on the same back lot meaning that different western productions overlapped; incredibly, they often used the same sets. And it wasn't just the actors they messed with; early on, there was a writers' strike, so instead of shutting down, the studio hired a mysterious scab writer to write during the strike. "W. Hermanos" was a prolific, albeit plagiaristic, writer of western scripts. It was only when I recognized the similarity between a *Maverick* script and a *Lawman* script did I realize what "W. Hermanos" really meant.

It was Spanish for "Warner Brothers."

Yes, the studio even had the gall to take a script from one show, make a few minor tweaks, and then reuse it for another. Screw the writers; it was anything to save a buck.

Warner Brothers also squeezed everything they could out of their actors: personal appearances (for which they took half), recordings, and photo dates with Warner starlets. I must admit, I didn't really mind that last one so much.

I did do a lot of appearances by myself; I seemed to have a special relationship with the young female audience. I have no idea how many personal appearances I made all over the country, but it was a lot. The fan mail that poured in was like an avalanche. Bags of it nearly filled up my little dressing room.

The actors I met on the show were incredible: Sammy Davis Jr., Kurt Russell, Ray Danton, L.Q. Jones. Peggie Castle played Miss Lily, the Bird Cage saloon owner and love interest for the marshal, replacing Bek Nelson who was the original actress playing the role. I adored Peggie; she was a super lady and a good actress who was always very professional. She was a great fit for the cast. Unfortunately, Peggie died at the age of forty-five, far too young.

I also met Robert Fuller, one of the greatest guys ever, on a *Lawman* episode entitled "The Friend." Appropriately, we've been "friends" ever since. Robert went on to star in Revue Studios' cowboy classic on NBC, *Laramie*, and stayed in the business for fifty-years. Married to the marvelous actress, Jennifer Savidge, he now lives on a ranch in Texas where I often visit.

When I watch television today with all its one-hour dramas, I think back and wonder what we, with our half-hour format, could have accomplished with double the amount of airtime. I mean, a half-hour drama is virtually unheard of today. *Lawman* required a tight story with rarely any secondary plot lines. There was little chance for me to romance the ladies or for any other characters to become really developed. The half-hour format just allowed John and me to develop our characters and their relationship while weekly presenting a good story. That pretty much consisted of catching the bad guys.

Lawman ran for four seasons. I was still fired up to do the show at the beginning of the fifth season. The ratings had been good; despite the large number of Westerns on TV at the time, we held our own, even when going up against the CBS juggernaut, *The Ed Sullivan Show*. We had been as high as number fifteen in our second season and consistently scored high in the Nielsen ratings. However, the studio, the omnipotent and intellectually challenged studio, wanted to change our time and day. And that was the beginning of the end.

We might easily have continued our run if not for the fact that ABC was infatuated with movies on television, prime-time television. They wanted a two-hour movie run on Sunday nights. There was the usual back-and-forth between our producers and the studio, but I felt they'd eventually get it figured out. I mean, I was twenty-six. . . I knew it all!

Or maybe not.

When our producers were offered a less desirable time-slot by the network, they screamed and bitched. Unfortunately for us, the R.J. Reynolds Tobacco Company owned *Lawman*, not our producers. Camel Cigarettes had all the commercials on our show, and Camel Cigarettes wanted to put on a movie instead of one of the best westerns of the day. The studio and the tobacco company couldn't seem to agree on a different time and date, so they did what geniuses of the time did:

They canceled the show.

I was dumbstruck as was the rest of the cast. All the actors cried. We had done one hundred and fity-six shows: thirty-nine

Peter Brown with *Lawman* co-stars, John Russell and Peggie Castle.

shows a year for four years, almost double what a modern series runs. And now it was over. Our last episode aired on October 2, 1962. *Lawman* was then put out to pasture.

During my time on the show, I had done guest appearances on other Warner Brothers' cowboy shows, sometimes as my character, Deputy Johnny McKay, and sometimes as a new character. One of the shows I was a guest on, *Maverick*, was a favorite of mine. Our two shows, in my inestimable opinion, were the best of what Warners had to offer in the western genre. Whereas *Lawman* was a serious western with just a few light moments, *Maverick* was a light western with just a few serious moments. I loved the change.

My last appearance on *Maverick* featured the crossover guest-cameo which was common in Warners' repertoire of gimmicky promotions. In that episode, Bart Maverick seeks help from some other Warners' stars. The show opened with the *Maverick* logo but with our theme song, I suppose to further identify *Lawman*. They then used our famous opening in which John tosses a rifle to me. As usual, I checked it and then sighted it. Only this time, Bart, played by Jack Kelly, approached the window. His expression turns to one of total fear as he thinks I'm aiming at him.

It was wonderfully, yet fleetingly, funny, somehow unsatisfying. It would have been a cute bit had Warner not promoted it so heavily ahead of time. It was like they were promising that we were going to be an integral part of the show, not just a "one-shot" joke. Of course by then, Warners had fallen back on one of their gimmicks, their standard procedure whenever one of their shows was experiencing troubles. And at that time, *Maverick* had a big problem.

His name was James Garner.

Now I loved working with *Maverick* star James Garner; any actor did. And in time, Jim and I became good friends. Not only was he an incredible actor, as his character "Bret Maverick" carried the show, but he could do so many other things so very well. His abilities as a card shark were not very far from Maverick's. And he was a fine softball player. I also liked to play softball, so I joined his team, "The UJI's," short for "United Jewish Italians."

The UJI had some other fine celebrity players. Crooner Bobby Darin played shortstop for us while fellow actor and good buddy Michael Dante roamed the outfield. With my strong arm, I played outfield and some first-base while James was our pitcher. Let me tell you, he was good . . . very good! We played Saturdays at Barrington Park between Sunset and Wilshire Boulevard in Los Angeles. Jim and I figured out that we were the sole "United" players on the team since we were the only ones who were neither Italian nor Jewish.

My guest appearances on the one-hour westerns like *Maverick* and *Cheyenne* took six days to shoot; the half-hour *Lawman* did it in only three. I'd usually get a script three to four days in advance and then I'd work on it at home. That way, I could come to the set on Monday morning and hit the ground running.

On *Maverick*, the six days afforded the cast a fair amount of free time. And free time for James meant playing cards. I was in a card game with him, L.Q. Jones, and some extras during the period between takes. We were having a good time, laughing and making fun of each other. I'm sure we were loud, probably louder than we should have been. Les Martinson, the director, had a reputation for always being behind schedule. This day, apparently, was no different.

Finally, after one particularly loud ruckus kicked up by us, he had had enough of our tomfoolery. Stomping over to the card table, he glared at Jim as he tried to formulate his words. Being the new guy on the set, I tried to make myself as small as possible.

"All right! All of you! Off my set! NOW!"

"Off your set?" replied Jim.

"You heard me! I want no more levity on my set!"

The stage went silent. A smile slowly crossed Jim's face, the star's face.

"Oh, no more levity?" he said as he rose to his feet. "Come on, boys. Let's move this game to my dressing room."

Slowly, we all got up and followed Jim out as Martinson looked on in disbelief. I'll give him this: he was a fair director . . . but still a royal pain in the ass. I guess pre-planning and communication just weren't his thing.

Jim was a good guy, but he wasn't averse to giving people and studios a hard time, especially if he felt they were trying to take advantage of him. Once he had a dispute with Warner Brothers. There was a strike on, so nobody was getting paid. Only, Jim, in his divine wisdom, had a fifty-two-week guarantee written into his contract, and he held Warners to it. A lawsuit ensued. Jim decided to stick it to the studio a bit more during the strike, so he gave me the key to his studio-supplied bungalow.

"I can't take your key," I said. "The studio —"

"Screw the studio!" he ordered. "Just move in. Don't ask them if it's all right. They don't have the balls to mess with you."

"But, but —"

"Just . . . move . . . in! They won't even notice."

So I did . . . and they didn't. It turned out to be a lovely place to spend my off-hours.

In the end, Garner's contract lawsuit with Warners was just before the start of the new *Maverick* season. Unfortunately for Warners, Jim won the suit; Warners had indeed violated his contract. Jim never came back to the show.

Good for Jim; bad for the viewing public.

Although it was fairly commonplace for other Warners' stars such as Clint Walker, Edd Byrnes, and Wade Preston to stage job actions of some type, I never joined in. It just wasn't my style. However, with the way Warners treated its stars, I don't think anyone would have blamed me had I done so.

My last exchange with James Garner didn't turn out so well for me. He had a business manager, Irving Leonard, that he swore by. Jim felt I needed a business manager and he thought Irving was the just the guy for me.

"How can you go wrong?" he said. "He's an Italian Jew."

Well, apparently I could go wrong. Three years later, I found out that, among other things, Irving had failed to file any IRS forms for me for the entire three years of our association. It took me quite a while to convince the government that I had not been out to cheat them. Needless to say, Irving was no longer on my payroll.

When *Lawman* ended in 1962, I was set to finish out my Warners' contract. I did quite a few guest appearances on some of their non-western series such as *Hawaiian Eye*, *77 Sunset Strip*, and *The Gallant Men*. I also did an excellent movie for Warners, *Merrill's*

Marauders, followed by a few for Disney and a beach flick, *Ride the Wild Surf*. But I was now ready for the next major event of my career. It came soon enough, although it included a change of employers.

Universal, a rival of Warners', also competed in the cowboy television market. They had a lot of success with long-running series such as *Bonanza* and *The Virginian*. Now they were going to branch out further into the western realm with their newest show, *Laredo*, a series of tales about the legendary Texas Rangers.

Whereas *Lawman* was a classic western, *Laredo* was at the other end of the drama spectrum. It was portrayed as a comedy western. *Laredo* maintained a consistently lighter tone than most shoot-'em-ups. It was very similar to the *Bonanza* episodes that didn't take themselves so seriously; the really funny one I remember about the Cartwright boys was when gigantic Hoss had to deal with leprechauns.

And I wasn't the only person who saw the similarities of the two shows. The network went so far as to air *Get Smart's* Don Adams doing the following promo for *Laredo*:

"What makes this hour-long series a sure winner is that '*Laredo*' has the same number of syllables as '*Bonanza*.'"

Not to toot my own horn (although this is my book, so if I don't do the "tootin'," who will?) but I was a hot property at the time. So hot, in fact, that in 1965 Universal bought my contract from Warners specifically so that I could be a lead in *Laredo*. It was like being a ballplayer and getting sent from the Yankees to the Dodgers.

Going to a rival production company gave me even more exposure. In addition to *Laredo*, I was able to make multiple guest appearances on Universal shows like *The Virginian*, *Wagon Train*, and *Kraft Suspense Theatre*. To me, it was all "business as usual."

In *Laredo*, I was to play "Chad Cooper, Texas Ranger." My two costars, also Texas Rangers, were William Smith as "Joe Riley" and Neville Brand as "Reese Bennett." I'm very close to William and at

(L-R) Peter Brown on the set of *Laredo* with William Smith and Neville Brand.

times still see him at Western shows. Phil Carey played our boss, "Captain Edward Parmalee." During the second season, they hired Robert Wolders to play another Ranger, "Erik Hunter." His character was quite the sophisticate with a Dutch accent, so the rest of our characters enjoyed making fun of his wardrobe and how he spoke. Robert and I actually did a show together in the somewhat recent past. He's such a likable gent. But really, all the fellas on the show got along.

The producers of *Laredo* wanted our characters to have the same kind of relationship and camaraderie as Cary Grant, Victor McLaglen, and Douglas Fairbanks, Jr. had in that big screen classic, *Gunga Din*, so that became the basis of our show. They had us watch it three times so that we could really recreate the relation-

31

ships. I immediately identified with Cary Grant's role as the romantic lead; William saw himself more as Douglas Fairbanks. That left Neville as Victor McLaglen, the comedian.

The Reese Bennett character, as portrayed by Neville, was a riot to play against. Basically, Chad Cooper and Joe Riley would take advantage of Reese. If he was sinking, we'd let him go down and then help him when he came back up. In other words, if Reese was in trouble, we'd let him be at first because he'd probably get out of it. But if he was in real trouble, we'd come to his aid. It was a very funny premise.

Neville Brand was a genuine character and a brilliant actor. Who else could have created "Reese Bennett" while never allowing the viewer to separate "the actor" from "the act." He was a most unusual man, wonderful in so many ways, but then not so great in others. He had been a platoon sergeant in World War II and had been one hell of a soldier, earning a silver star for gallantry in combat. That honor was earned when his unit was under intense fire from a German machine gun nest hunkered down in a hunting lodge. Neville worked his way around behind the command post/lodge, burst in through the rear, and single-handedly captured the enemy inside. He received numerous other awards and citations, including a Purple Heart for being shot in the arm and nearly bleeding to death during action near the Weser River in Germany.

The flip side to this brave yet violent man was his love of children. One day a family came on the set. Their ten-year-old daughter spotted Neville and raced up to him, throwing her arms around his waist and giving him a big hug. When he picked her up, she kissed his cheek.

"I think they should change the name of the show," she announced. "Instead of *Laredo*, they should call it The Reese Bennett Show."

Neville hugged her back, then wiped his eyes as he set her down. "Thanks, honey," he said softly.

Bill Smith and I overheard this exchange. We looked at each other and knew that Neville was done for the day. He immediately left the set. We didn't know whether or not Neville had witnessed some atrocity to kids in the war, but for whatever reason, they always had this effect on him.

Neville was hugely impacted by that war. It was probably a major cause of his excessive drinking. Because of his eccentric behavior, it was rumored that Universal had hired Robert at the start of the second season so that if there were problems with Neville, they'd have a substitute already on the set. There was other talk of the studio replacing him with Albert Salmi or Claude Akins, but in the end, they thought better of that. After all, it would be quite the public relations disaster to fire a highly decorated American war hero. Still, Neville didn't make it easy on the higher-ups.

Universal ran a tour through the studios and the back lot many times a day. A lead car pulling five to seven open-air trams gave about about 200 tourists an inside-look at the goings-on of a major television and movie operation. A guide up front described all the sights by the use of a booming loudspeaker system.

Unfortunately for us, the tram ran right by our dressing rooms. Although it was nice for the public and provided the studio with another source of income, the continual invasion of privacy and the constant din of the various guides blithering on about this and that got to wear on our nerves. And it bothered no one more than it did Neville. He was the one who ultimately did something about it, complaining to the suits in the Black Tower, actor-speak for the executive wing of the company. He asked them more than once to re-route the tram. Their response was an unequivocal, non-debatable "No!" every time.

That type of response did not play well with Neville. He finally took matters into his own hands. Late one morning as the tram went by with its guide spewing forth his usual drivel, Neville stood in the doorway of his dressing room, smiling and waving at all the moms and dads and kids. But then, before anyone knew what was happening, Neville made his complaint known publicly in a way only Neville could:

He dropped his trousers and began taking a leak.

Screams and gasps echoed throughout the building, but Neville just kept peeing away. His epic piss-off lasted the entire length of the studio tour tram, right down to the last car. Oh, there were threats of suspension and fines from upstairs, but Neville just laughed them off. And needless to say, the studio rerouted the tram the next day.

I enjoyed doing *Laredo*, especially being as comfortable as I was with my horse. I continued to use *Houdini*. Beyond being good at the usual things you need a picture horse to be good at, he had one other special talent that I absolutely loved: he could jump over the

Laredo Cast (L-R) Phil Carey as Captain Edward Parmalee; Peter Brown as Texas Ranger Chad Cooper; Neville Brand as Texas Ranger Reese Bennett; William Smith as Texas Ranger Joe Riley.

moon.

In one episode, *Houdini* was supposed to bound over a burning hay wagon. The director had his assistant bring in a stuntman and a stunt horse. Unfortunately, when they did a trial run, the stunt horse balked; he would not jump over the burning wagon. I saw a solution so I approached the harried director.

"We can do it," I said.

"Who can do what?" he dryly replied.

"The jump. *Houdini* and I can make that jump. My horse doesn't know what "stop" is."

"Are you kidding me?" the director said, more a statement than a question. "Do you know what kind of trouble I'd be in if something happened to the star and his horse during that jump? I'd be back directing kiddie shows on local TV. I can't let you do it."

I was persistent, however.

"No way are you going to get the shot you want without my horse," I said matter-of-factly.

He considered my words. Finally, he relented, somewhat.

"OK, here's what I'm going to do. I'm breaking for lunch. I'm not going to be anywhere near this set. I have a feeling that the cinematographer will keep the film rolling. I'm not ordering it, but it just might happen. Do you get me?"

Oh, I got him.

The director gave me a quick wink, then turned and headed for the commissary. As soon as he did, I mounted *Houdini*, rode down to the other end of the street, and then turned and took off at full speed right at the burning wagon. Just as I could feel the heat of the fire on my face, *Houdini* elevated, soaring well over the flames, and landed oh-so gently on the other side.

WE DID IT!

I turned back to the cinematographer who gave me the high sign that he had gotten the shot. I dismounted, got *Houdini* to the watering trough, and then also broke for lunch. It was all in a day's work for Chad Cooper, Texas Ranger.

Working with horses was a delight for me. Working with the regular cast was enjoyable. And working with most guest stars was usually fun, but not always. The one guest on the set I had trouble liking was a man who gained great fame on another show. Lieutenant Steve McGarrett on *Hawaii Five-0* was a great character; the man who played him, Jack Lord, maybe not so much, at least in my estimation.

Lord had gained his initial fame several years earlier as "Felix Leiter" in the first James Bond movie, *Dr. No.* He was eventually replaced in the film series when he demanded more money, an increase in the size of his role, and, incredibly, costar billing with Sean Connery. Sean Connery! That gives you the kind of idea of the arrogance of this guy.

I will give you that he was quite the philanthropist in later years, but as an actor he was known as an anal-retentive perfectionist. That's not always a bad thing, but in his case, his control-freak nature made him a very disliked actor. I remember nothing positive about him.

Jack was with us just once on *Laredo* for an episode titled "*Above the Law.*" One day I noticed Jack and a stunt-cowboy in the distance; he was riding his horse on the back lot while the cowboy seemed to be giving him lessons. That seemed strange, because Jack had quite a background doing cowboy shows: *Have Gun, Will Travel*; *Gunsmoke*; *Rawhide*; *Bonanza*; *Wagon Train*. Plus, he had the lead in the short-lived rodeo cowboy series, *Stoney Burke.* I don't know; maybe he didn't have to ride horses in those shows, because he was sure enough having trouble here. It was as if he couldn't even get on the horse.

My mistake was going down there and offering him what I thought was some well-needed help.

"You have to get on and off the horse more smoothly," I offered.

Jack immediately took offense.

"Hey!" he exclaimed. "I sure as hell don't need your help!"

"Sorry," was all I could say.

I tipped my hat and then rode away, suitably chastened. We rarely spoke the rest of the week.

In general, *Laredo* had pretty good ratings, but our 8:30-9:30 p.m. Thursday night time slot in competition with *Bewitched*, *My Three Sons*, and *The Thursday Night Movie* made it tough to score too high in the Nielsen ratings. Our numbers after moving to 10 p.m. on Fridays were even worse. *Laredo* was on the air for just two years. The show had a lot of potential, but it definitely struggled to find its footing. But it brings back good memories for me, and it's still recalled fondly by many of my fans as evidenced by their comments to me at my appearances at western shows.

I didn't realize it at the time that the era of the cowboy show was nearing its end. I think deep down in my gut, though, I knew that the westerns I so loved would soon be gone from television and movies; my cowboy days were pretty much done. It was with a heavy heart that I put my guns and hat in storage. But the most difficult entity to part with caused me a huge regret. It was time to let go of an old friend who meant the world to me: my horse, *Houdini*.

Yes, I had finally come to the decision to sell my *Lawman/Laredo* mount. However, something caused me to change my mind. I had watched the teen-age girl trainer who used to exercise the show's horses. She was so good with them, especially doing practice jumps. Then when I found out she had no horse of her own, my heart just melted. I liked the idea of *Houdini* going to someone who would really care about him, so I made the momentous decision to offer my trusty steed to the young lady. She was ecstatic about the gift. It was like losing a child when I watched her lead him out of the horse barn for the last time.

I had managed to do a lot of guest shots on other westerns including before, after, and in-between my two series, but by the end of *Laredo*, that genre was virtually gone. Looking back, I thankfully got to play two wonderful and diverse characters: the eager-to-please, brave, innocent (at least with the women) Deputy Johnny McKay in *Lawman*; and the confident, also brave, charming (but scheming) womanizing Texas Ranger Chad Cooper in *Laredo*. The cowboy chapter of my life had come to a close. But I knew one thing for sure:

The rest of the book called "my life" had a long way to go.

WHY TELEVISION MUST REFORM ITSELF, OR ELSE...

By Henry Steele Commager see page 6

LOCAL PROGRAMS • JUNE 25-JULY 1

TV GUIDE

15¢

WILLIAM SMITH, PETER BROWN, PHILIP CAREY, NEVILLE BRAND OF 'LAREDO'

Laredo cast on the cover of *TV Guide*.

"Now how am I ever going to be a cowboy?!"
-My reaction when told about the
family's move to California

Chapter 2
My Family

I never knew my father . . . my biological father, that is. John Patton de Lappe was a journalist for the Hearst Corporation. I have virtually no recollection of him as he died when I was only four. I was told the following apocryphal story:

He went out one morning to get the Sunday paper, contracted pneumonia, and died shortly thereafter.

I don't believe a lick of it.

I had a sister, Joan, five years older than me who was also a mystery. It's hard to believe but she and I met only two times during our lives. As an adult, I met with Joan and Ethel de Lappe, my grandmother, in Beverly Hills. Joan had been raised for the most part by her paternal grandparents. What I thought would be a joyous reunion, however, turned out to be a most unsettling confrontation. Ethel was not friendly at all. I'm sure it had something to do with John's relationship with my mother. Or, maybe she was just a grumpy old lady. Either way, I walked out the door and never looked back. It was the second and final time I ever saw my sister Joan. She passed away in 2005 having never reconnected with the family. More's the pity.

I was born in Manhattan at the Sloane Baby Hospital on October 5, 1935. You may recall (OK, probably not) that on Christmas Day, 1899, Humphrey Bogart was also born at Sloane.

Here's another interesting tidbit from "Peter's Fountain of Fun Facts": According to the last census, October 5th is the most common birthday in the United States. It's probably because a lot of people are getting busy in order to stay warm in January, thus making for a lot of us "Libras" to be born in October.

And you thought you weren't going to learn anything reading this book?

When John Patton de Lappe died, my mom "Mina," short for "Wilhelmina," held it together for my older brother Phil and me. Eventually, I got that strong male influence that was so important to growing boys like me. His name was Albert Henry Brown.

Just before World War II, Mom met Albert, the man who was to become my stepfather. Albert and Mina both worked for the Grumman Aircraft Engineering Corporation, a leading producer of military and civilian aircraft. The factory was in Northport, Long Island. Grumman had designed the first practical float with a retractable landing gear for the navy, and this had launched Grumman into the aviation market. During World War II, they became known for their Navy fighter aircraft: the F4F Wildcat, the F6F Hellcat, and, for its torpedo bomber, the TBF Avenger. Years later at a viewing of the movie *Top Gun*, I felt an immense sense of pride when I saw Grumman products prominently being used.

Albert, also known as "Bud," was a Chief Inspector at Grumman. The company was forward thinking enough that they employed women back then. I'm sure they knew the war was coming and there'd be a shortage of men.

My energetic mother began working there after my father passed away, and before long, everyone there knew her. She was like the original "Rosie the Riveter."

Bud saw her around and started calling her "Red" due to her striking auburn hair. The two of them began meeting for coffee

Peter with his Mom and Dad on the *Laredo* set.

every day along with a mutual friend named Steve. They used to flip coins to see who would buy. For some reason, Mom lost every time. She couldn't figure it out. Months later, she learned why she was the one always doling out for the coffee: Steve and Bud were using two-headed nickels.

There was no doubt where this blossoming relationship was heading; Red and Bud were married in 1940. Bud absolutely adored Mina, right up until the day she passed from this Earth. They're both gone now.

Although I acquired my inspiration to be in show business from my mom, it was from my stepfather that I learned the importance of a strong work ethic. He was so accomplished and such a great athlete. He was a champion boxer in the navy, played baseball for the New York Giants in their farm system, and was a world class speed skater. This guy could do it all. In one race, he finished a close second to eventual U.S. Skating Hall of Famer Irving Jaffee. Jaffee had been the winner of two gold medals at the Lake Placid Winter Olympics in 1932. I remember Bud had a plaque with at least a dozen speed skating medals on it. He was very proud of them.

Phil and I knew we liked this guy a lot, so we didn't want to screw it up. We were in the Northport house at 408 Woodbine on Long Island when we had our first big argument concerning Bud. It happened the day after the wedding.

Come to think of it, it was two arguments. Phil and I first disagreed about what we were going to call Albert; it came down to either "Dad" or "Pop." After we finally settled on "Pop," we then tried to figure out who was going to call him "Pop" first. As the oldest, Phil said he was the boss and that he had decided I should do it. Not completely sure about this little bit of fraternal tyranny, I protested vehemently.

"Who knows if he even wants to be our "Pop"?" I argued.

In the end, we decided we would say it together. "Pop" beamed when he heard our little rehearsed duet. And when I got ready to go to school that fall, Mom took me aside and said, "This year when they ask you at school, you tell them you're "Peter Brown."

And so I was.

Being Peter Brown was fine by me. Phil and I were both soon adopted by Pop and legally took the name "Brown." That really helped to solidify the family and Phil and my relationship with him. Unlike the stereotypical stories you hear about abusive step-parents, Pop never hit us kids. In retrospect, we didn't need much discipline. He loved Mom so much and that, in turn, made us respect him all the more. There was no disconnect between the new man in the house and his two now stepsons. We loved him right away and would not have wanted to do anything to disappoint him. I carried that thought with me long into my career.

We soon also learned what a knowledgeable current-events

My mother, Wilhelmina "Mina" Helen Reaume Brown

minded man he was; World War II was a major concern of his. On our living room wall he painted a huge map of the world so that he could keep track of and explain every event that was going on in the war. He would use pins and string to follow troop movements, pulling information from the newspapers as well as the radio. He really wanted his boys to be aware of what was going on in the world. I have nothing but fond memories of Pop.

Mom was very supportive of all this and joined in with the constant updating of the war map. Mom did it all and always with a smile. She was very easy to get along with. If you needed a hand, she'd be the first one there to help. If you needed money, she'd give it to you with a smile. Of course, she was no easy mark: she did expect to be paid back and would let you know if you were in arrears. As Frank Sinatra might say, "She was a broad in the best sense of the word." My description of her was more like the song "Honey Bun" from *South Pacific*: "She's broad where a broad should be broad."

Phil and I always had a good relationship, but that's not to say we were perfect angels. After all, we were brothers. We grew up in a more rural time on Long Island, if you can believe that. Our house was right on Long Island Sound; the boardwalk practically ran through our backyard. We had a party line. There was a barn across the street. Sounds like *The Real McCoys*, doesn't it?

I was a sports-oriented kid who stayed very active. We had a long, long driveway that took forever to shovel in the winter. We used to get on a sled together and go flying down the driveway onto the ice. There was a pier across the street from which Phil and I would fish on many weekends. We'd usually come home with a flounder or two. Sometimes, we'd traipse into town, just the two of us. Of course, that would never happen nowadays. Inevitably, Phil would get distracted and then head home leaving me behind. That happened many times.

Probably our worst boyhood scrum came the day Phil threw all my clothes out the window of our bedroom, our second floor bedroom. Being the genius I was, I stupidly climbed out the window to retrieve my wardrobe and immediately fell through the roof . . . the glass roof! I slammed down onto a workbench below, glass flying everywhere. Like a Rube Goldberg machine, the force of my fall rocked the workbench enough that it tipped over a shovel that had been leaning against the wall; in turn, the shovel tipped over and bonked me square in the head.

All was quiet for a moment. I lay there stunned as blood trickled down my forehead. Phil took one look and, like any intelligent big brother, got the hell out of there. It was not a good day for Peter. And it only got worse when Mom walked in. She let out a shriek that was somewhere between terrified and just really pissed off.

My mom, Wilhelmina "Mina" Helen Reaume Brown, was a Christmas Eve baby born in 1906. An accomplished radio and stage actress, she was the first model for me of how to go about working in show business. My earliest memories of Mom are of her involvement in the entertainment world, mostly on the radio. Mom was "The Dragon Lady" on the famous *Terry and the Pirates*

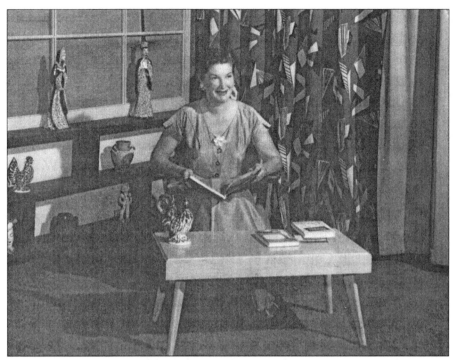

My mother on the set of her radio show.

show. She also hosted a kids' program called *Let's Pretend*. As a little boy, I enjoyed going to the studio; by age six, I began appearing on the radio with her. I think my first speaking part was on the *Let's Pretend* show.

By this time, another addition to the family had come along: my half-brother Mike. I don't know how Mom did it, but she continued to do her radio shows, even then with three rambunctious boys in tow. Fortunately for Mom, Phil and I had been bitten by the acting bug. We both worked on *Let's Pretend*, playing small parts such as elves or fairies. Phil remembers as a little boy walking down that shiny brown floor with the gold stripes in the RCA Building hand-in-hand with Mom. A half-a-lifetime later when he worked for NBC, he walked down the same hallway, his memory immediately reverting back to those times with her.

Brother Phil is three years older than me. Being the elder, he had more chances than I did to be on the radio. He did a second show: *The Bill Fairwood Show* which, amazingly enough, Pop wrote while Mom directed. Phil played the part of "Moosenose" in a cast with a bunch of other teenagers. It aired on station KROW in Oakland. Phil did the "Playground News" segment which consisted of him reporting on highlights of what was going on in the world of kids. Boy, what I wouldn't give now to have a copy of that tape. Phil ended up as Director of Sports Operations -West Coast for NBC. Not bad, big brother!

When the war started, there were big changes coming for the newly minted Brown family. Pop got a job transfer to the Grumman plant in California in 1942. The way they broke the news to us kids was most interesting.

It's still a little foggy to me, but Phil says it was the middle of the night when Pop and Mom, then pregnant with my youngest brother Paul, woke us up from sound sleeps and simply said, "We're leaving." There was no warning, no earthly sign that we were preparing to abandon the house, much less go all the way across the country. It was like a college initiation prank and we were the pledges being given just minutes to pack before being hustled out of the house. A cab was waiting in the pitch-black night; off it sped, not stopping until it slammed on the brakes in front of the train station.

When we arrived in Chicago, we had to change trains. In a move that would make present day Child Protective Services personnel shudder, Mom and Pop left 10-year-old Phil alone in the station to watch the luggage while they took Mike and me to find our connection. Well, things must have been pretty confusing, because as Phil puts it, "You guys never came back!"

After an hour or so, a porter came up to my big brother.

"Are you Phil?" he asked.

The youngster shifted uneasily from foot to foot while hesitating about talking to a stranger, a black stranger.

"Yes," he finally said meekly. The porter rolled his eyes.

Mom and Pop had forgotten Phil!

I don't know if years of therapy were ever going to be enough to allow Phil to come to terms with that abandonment. The best I can say is, he survived.

The porter grabbed the bags and rushed Phil over to another train. The train the rest of us were on had been forced to stop up ahead so that Phil's train could catch up and reunite the family. Phil was in tears as my mom did her best to comfort him. To me, however, I didn't see what the big fuss was. It was just part of this most grand adventure.

The near-loss of Phil wasn't the end of the incidents on "The Train Ride to Neverland." Somewhere along the line, an inebriated sailor tried to hit on my mom, my very pregnant mom. You remember I told you that Pop was a champion boxer in the navy? Well, even this many years later, he hadn't lost a step . . . uh, "punch." One right-cross later, Pop was still the the undefeated navy boxing champion.

As the train whistled through the night, Mom finally leveled with me.

"Peter," she said, "we're going out west."

That's great! I thought. *Absolutely great!*

I had been a big fan of *The Lone Ranger* show on the radio, so that's what I thought our lives were now going to be like: horses, wild Indians, shooting at bad guys. I quickly sounded off, asking about places I hoped we were going.

"Texas?! Arizona?! New Mexico?!"

I tried to come up with anything that sounded western to me. Mom looked away pensively. Then in that quiet, comforting manner that all moms have, she tried to explain the way of the world to me.

"No, Peter, we're not going to Texas, Arizona, or New Mexico. We're going west . . . to California. That's where your dad's new job is located."

I stared at her disbelievingly.

"California!?" I shouted. "California's not west!"

She rolled her eyes, knowing that an argument at this inopportune time with a six-year old would be futile. She leaned back and tried to go to sleep. I, on the other hand, was too exasperated to sleep. I stared out the window at the fast-moving fields rushing by.

California?! I thought. *Now how am I ever going to be a cowboy?!*

There were more surprises in store when we finally got to our destination. None of our stuff ever made it to California. Somewhere on that trip, everything disappeared, whether it had been during the unfortunate change of trains or if some light-fingered bad guy had made off with our worldly possessions.

Phil pointedly spoke up, saying, "It wasn't me! I was the one watching the luggage!"

Our first stop was Hunter's Point at 437 Eagle Avenue. I don't know why, but I have an incredible memory for the addresses of all the places I've lived. I may not be able to remember what I had for breakfast yesterday, but I sure as shootin' can remember addresses.

Hunter's Point was O.K. back then; today it's much worse. We lived in one of those cracker-box houses, old family units intended for enlisted personnel. We didn't stay there very long. We soon became residents at the Alameda Naval Air Station.

Mom and Pop both worked as inspectors. Amazingly enough, they became friends with this really wacky lady there. She always referred to her husband as "Fang." The "she" I'm talking about, of course, turned out years later to be the great comedienne Phyllis Diller.

The war dragged on. Finally, in August of 1945, while Pop, Phil, and I were off in a rowboat fishing the Russian River, we noticed everyone on shore had begun cheering and screaming and the air-raid sirens were going off. We soon learned that the Japanese had surrendered. World War II was over!

By that time, we were living in Coarsegold, California. Our detour there had been a result of Pop's deteriorating health. It turned out that he couldn't handle the heat, something that would have been nice to know before moving to the sweat box called "California." His doctor offered him the option of either moving to the mountains or else going back to New York City. Pop, never one to retreat, proceeded to rent a 4,000-acre ranch in the Sierra Nevada Mountains.

Now, one might wonder what we would do with or how we could afford such a massive place. But before you get too worked up over it, just know that 3,000 of those acres were straight up and down.

What I remember best about the ranch was that it was the place where I really learned how to ride a horse. The property had belonged to a real cowboy who just happened to have made his way into show business. I'm talking about that great old character actor, Slim Pickens. I can still see him riding that atomic bomb like a bucking bronco in the groundbreaking film, *Dr. Strangelove*.

In the great room in the main house on the ranch, there was a huge stone fireplace with a thick, thick slab of roughly hewn oak as a mantelpiece. So many times I sat in that room and looked at the letters carved into the mantel: a sideways "2" followed by "2P".

What the hell does that mean? I thought so many times.

It took quite a few years, but my question was finally answered two states away. I was on a publicity junket for a company that was building six golf courses in Washington state. They were doing a promotion with celebrities to get people to buy homes on the courses. I was not only being paid to do this, but they were also giving me a plot of land near where they were building. Having no real use for it at the time, I eventually gave it to my *Lawman* co-star, John Russell.

For the junket, the company sent a helicopter to take a bunch of us up to the property. Once aboard, I realized that Slim Pickens was one of the other celebs. Now was my chance to have my question answered, so I quickly introduced myself.

"Slim, I'm Peter Brown," I eagerly said. "Back when I was growing up, I think I lived on your ranch."

"You lived on my ranch," he replied with a big smile. "Which one?"

"In Coarsegold, California."

"That's my place," he beamed.

"Slim, I got to know: what was the lettering for on your fireplace mantel? You know, the "two on its side" followed by another "2" and the letter "P"?

He rubbed his chin in thought, then began to laugh.

"Son, that's my name for the ranch. It's our brand."

"Yeah, but what did it stand for?"

"Just like it reads: Too Lazy To Pee!"

That cracked up everyone on the helicopter.

Slim's ranch had one horse, an old gray mare named *Diamond*. To Phil and me, however, he was a dashing steed, our transportation to anywhere. Being the clever boys we were, we changed his name to *Dime*.

Now we were really out in the wild west. Our school, Sierra Union High, had an enrollment that was seventy percent American Indian. And to get to school, we had to take a . . . wait for it . . . SEVENTY-THREE-MILE BUS RIDE! In addition to the two-hour, each-way, time-I'll-never-get-back-in-my-life bus ride, we had a one-hour walk from home to the bus stop. I'm not sure the child-cruelty laws were in effect back then.

Fortunately, we had our trusty ride, *Dime*, to lessen the load. Each day we rode him to town to pick up the bus, leaving him in a rental barn while we furthered our "higher" education. Once on the bus, we figured out that the only way to make those marathon rides bearable was to have a girlfriend. So, I looked around and soon enough, Darlene Kampman became my bus-buddy, junior high girlfriend.

I liked school. I was a pretty good student, just not in Latin (Although, again, while I sometimes can't even remember what I did yesterday, for some reason I can still recite *Gallia est omnes divisa in partes tres.*) Since I had a very strong arm, I played baseball. And amazingly enough, I learned to cook at school, although not from any of the established curriculum. It stemmed, however, from an ulterior motive of mine.

The school served hot lunches everyday, so they often needed help in the cafeteria. The head cook (I refuse to call her a "chef") owned a young horse that she wanted to sell. Since I had no money, I offered her the following deal: In exchange for my time working in the kitchen each day, she agreed to give me her horse.

And that's how I acquired "*Pronto*," a roan gelding. *Pronto* was the first horse I ever owned, so I rode him a lot. Besides, that was a necessary step in my lifelong march towards full cowboyhood.

These were hard times financially for the family, so everybody pitched in. Pop took a job at McMahan's Furniture store in Madera. Established in 1919, McMahan's was the oldest furniture store in the country, at least until it went out of business in 2008.

Phil, Mike, and I raked oak leaf mold to sell as fertilizer. We peddled the stuff door-to-door. I can tell you that was one hard-ass job; I hated doing it, breathing in the dust and all, which was even scarier when you consider that I was a longtime asthma sufferer. Fortunately from when I was a little shaver, I always had my inhaler, primitive as it was back in those days. Regardless, you do what you have to do to get by. Looking back on my youth, I did have my fair share of asthma scares, but it was just something I learned to live with.

With my lack of money, a big night out was having Pop take

Darlene and me to the drive-in movie. We would cuddle up under a blanket in the back of the truck and have our own kind of fun.

Our family finally moved off the ranch and back to civilization. I went to Coalinga High School in the San Joaquin Valley where I played baseball and softball. I even tried football but soon rethought my decision when I was at the bottom of a heap with a ton of guys piled on top of me. You see, I hadn't had my growth spurt yet. I was quite small then.

Fortunately, the football coach saw my predicament. Maybe he feared for my life. I don't know, but whatever it was, after taking a good look at my lack of size, he suggested I try tennis. That turned out to be some of the most sage advice ever offered to me.

Tennis served me well throughout my life. I became very good at it, even winning many celebrity events in later years. And I suffered no bone-crushing tackles while on the court. It became my game.

Besides athletics and my jobs, I did some other extracurriculars. Coalinga High was where I received my real indoctrination to the stage theater arts. And just as with tennis, my life was served very well with my early involvement with stage work. From then till now, I've never been far from one sort of theater or another.

I always had a part-time job in those years. I worked at a local gas station during high school. It wasn't that I was a nut for cars or anything, nor was I the kind of kid fascinated by carburetors or intake manifolds. Back then, you didn't need to be a grease monkey to work in a gas station. You just filled customer's tanks, cleaned their windshields, and checked their oil.

Yes, in those days, we checked their oil.

One day while I was working at the gas station, an earthquake hit. Being from New York, I wasn't sure what to do. I looked around and saw that the vibrations were shaking the tire rack high up on the wall. I didn't know exactly what was happening, but I did know that I needed to leave . . . now! Sure enough, the tires shook loose from the rack and began a rubber landslide headed directly at me. I did a bit of fancy open-field running as the stampede of rolling tires came after me.

I didn't make it to graduation in California. I mean, I did graduate, just not there. The family moved yet once again, this time to Spokane, Washington, where I would spend my senior year at North Central High.

Mom's hometown was Yakima; she had been a friend of Bing Crosby's there and had gone on to matriculate at Gonzaga University. I wasn't aware of it at the time, but my mom's family owned a pub in a small town in Oregon near a lake. Mom's sister lived nearby. This property had apparently been left to my mother and her sister and it had caused quite a rift between the two. The ownership dispute of that tavern was ultimately the reason we moved to Washington.

In Spokane, I joined a theater group and worked for a local drug store delivering prescriptions. Phil was out of the army by then and was working at a Shell gas station.

Mom continued with her entertainment career, this time in television. She was the host of a local Spokane show called *Lady Fair*, a daytime ladies' program which included a lot of interviews. Her most memorable guest was the dog expert who brought several animals to appear on the show. When Mom asked about the pedigree of a certain dog, the guest responded, "Her father was a sire from San Francisco and the mother was a bitch from Tacoma."

Mom sat there speechless with a shocked expression. The mail poured in the next day.

I graduated from high school in January of 1953 at the ripe old age of 17. At North Central, advanced learners had the opportunity to graduate after the first semester of their senior year, so by January, I was ready to don my cap and gown.

Now as I just said, I was never far away from theater; stardom

High School Photo

Brown, Peter Lynn
Social Studies
Transferred from Coalinga, California
News Staff

had been my goal for a long time. And while I used performances in theatrical productions to hone my acting skills, I ultimately wanted to be in the movies.

My job delivering prescriptions gave me a lot of time to ponder my future. After much thought and weighing many options about my goal of attaining stardom, I came up with a solution which I felt would be an incredible stepping stone toward achieving immortality in Hollywood.

I would enlist in the army.

Yes, you heard right; I decided to enlist in the army.

Now to the untrained eye, that might not appear to have been a brilliant career move. However in 1954, it made a lot of sense to this somewhat worldly teenager who had life completely figured out. I decided I would volunteer for the draft, which would mean a two-year commitment, whereas volunteering for the regular army was a three-year commitment. Then after putting in my time for two years, the army, via the largesse of the GI Bill, would happily pay for all my necessary education which would get me a star on the Hollywood Walk of Fame. More specifically, they would pay for me to attend the Leland Powers School of Radio, Television and Theatre in Boston.

I can tell you have another question:

Why would a person want to move to the east coast in order to become a star on the west coast?

Well, I didn't come upon this decision frivolously. An army buddy of mine, David Clasby, told me that Leland Powers was where he was going to attend, so I figured, *What the hell?* and that's where we both decided to go when we got out of the army.

Boy, talk about your angst-ridden, soul-searching, decision making processes.

Back then, the army had what was called "the buddy system." If you volunteered with a friend, the army said they would "try," that being the operative word, to keep you together. Strength in numbers, I guess. So, a pal of mine, Don Blair, and I decided we'd go into the service together. Although we were both in Spokane at the time, we decided to hitchhike to Don's family's place in San Diego and enlist there.

After making it through basic training at Fort Ord, California, the army, as is their way, sent Don to Germany and, being true to their word, shipped me to . . . Alaska?

Now wait just a darned minute!

You mean to tell me that while Don would be overseas sending me photos of all the beautiful German women he'd be dating, I'd be in that feared battlefield of the north, Ladd Air Force Base, Fairbanks, Alaska, trying to establish a lasting relationship with a moose? I don't think so. I demanded a refund, a do-over, anything that might improve my situation. The army didn't quite agree. Guess who won the debate?

Here's an interesting sidelight concerning Don that again shows just how lucky one man can be, that "one man" not being me. During my time in Spokane before I joined the army, I was dating a lovely young woman named Ginger Maher. We weren't engaged or anything, but I really did like this gal. Well, Don and I enlisted together, but he had the incredible fortune of coming home from boot camp two weeks before I did. Somehow, he and Ginger got together, fell in love, and were married three years later.

Actually, I was all right with that. In fact, about ten-years later, I was in San Jose with a group of friends for an all-star baseball game, so I invited Don and Ginger to go to dinner with my group which also included Joe Dimaggio and Doug McClure. It was an unforgettable time. Oh, I miss the Blairs.

Back to the service. I was a member of the army's Second Infantry Division. Although Ladd was an air base, army dopes like me were sent there as security for all the military personnel there. Yet oddly enough, I was not trained as an MP. The army, in its infinite wisdom, had made me a painter.

Yes, they made a soldier with a history of asthma a painter.

Ye gads!

Luckily, an air force doctor figured out my problem and removed me from painting duty. So now I needed to find something else to do before the army decided to use me as a projectile of some kind.

A couple of buddies and I were at the PX one night just sitting around bullshitting trying to decide what we could do to keep from freezing to death. I remembered an old adage my pop had taught me: Whenever you get stuck about what to do, find a need and fill it.

I thought about that for a bit and suddenly, as if Pop was in my head, it came to me: the need I found on the base that needed filling was . . . entertainment. I blurted it out to the guys, telling them about my background in radio working and acting with my mom and about my time as a high school thespian. Untypical of the guys, they did not shoot the idea down.

"We should put on some shows," I gushed, sounding to all the world like a typical Broadway plot of the day.

As it turned out, our small meeting that evening was a bit of kismet; the other two guys were not entertainment novices.

What are the odds?

Dick Deneut, whom I had known since basic training, had worked for Globe Photos in L.A. taking pictures of celebrities. Globe was a longtime company whose anti-paparazzi style had them working with, instead of against, the studios to promote their famous stars. Photos of celebs relaxing or cavorting in the surf with other big names were the order of the day at Globe.

After his time in the service, Dick went back to Globe for what would be a long and very successful career, eventually moving up to vice-president and West Coast bureau chief. In later years, he wrote actress Patricia Neal's autobiography, a TV movie, and he authored the wonderful coffee-table book, *Inside Hollywood: 60 Years of Globe Photos.* He was a perfect addition to our fledgling operation.

"Great idea!" Dick chimed in. "I can handle all promotions to get the word out about our shows!"

So Dick got put in charge of marketing.

"And I can be the producer," added our third partner, the afore-mentioned David Clasby from Boston.

Not just blowing smoke, David had experience producing stage plays back east and in Los Angeles at the Horseshoe Stage Theater. With him as producer and technical director, it was now all coming together.

That left the toughest and least glamorous jobs for me: lead actor and director. I know, I know, it's a dirty job, but somebody had to do it. Now all that was left was to get permission from someone and maybe then we could get the hell out of the freezing cold.

USO shows were infrequent in Fairbanks; after all, it's not exactly on the main route to . . . anywhere. Since my records did indeed show that I had an extensive background in the field of entertainment, I managed to wrangle an assignment to the base's theater group. I was going to work full time entertaining the men.

Somebody up there is looking out for me, I thought.

There was one smallish problem that I immediately determined could affect the quality of our shows: the base's theater group didn't actually exist.

But I wasn't Mina Brown's son for nothing. Not wanting to be put to work doing KP ("kitchen police" for the militarily-uninitiated), guard duty, or some other moronic job unique to my skill set, I right away took it upon myself, along with my two cohorts, to create a base theater group.

The general in charge of Ladd wasn't a big fan of the stage; he as much as said he thought it was a waste of valuable soldier-hours. Grudgingly, however, he bequeathed to our sturdy little entourage what he deemed to be a suitable theatrical facility; in reality, it was an ancient quonset hut being used solely for the storage of huge washers, dryers, and linens. Now pretty much abandoned, in better times they called it a "laundry facility."

At present, it was a dump.

Nobody was going to come there to see our shows. So, going against everything that Pop had taught me, I decided to lie, cheat, or steal, whatever was necessary to see that "the show must go on." I formulated a brilliant plan.

The base actually had both an army general and an air force general in charge. Through stealthy reconnaissance, I discovered that each of these multi-starred officers had a wife who loved the theater.

Who knew?

My first step then was to recruit the two stage-struck ladies to help us put on our first production, the stage classic comedy *Arsenic and Old Lace*. It was about two dotty sisters who liked to murder men and then bury them in the basement. Of course, both of the generals' wives were thrilled to be asked to play the leads. They, too, were looking for something to do on that Godforsaken air base. Well, you'd have thought we had offered them a ride to the moon. Without hesitation they said "Yes!"

Now here's where I got really clever. On the day I was to show them our "theater," I made sure the quonset hut/laundry facility/ rats' nest was looking extra dumpy. During the tour, I pretended to be thrilled with our theatrical accommodations, but as soon as the generals' wives saw where we would be performing, they were horrified.

"This is impossible!" one of them exclaimed.

"We can't work here! No way!" uttered the other.

After a quick confab, they "surprised" me by deciding the theater definitely needed an upgrade. I acted somewhat astonished at their assessment but quickly deferred to their judgment.

"Let us talk to our husbands," said the first one. "There's a new service club about to open. Maybe we can get their O.K. to use it."

"Ain't no 'maybe' about it," said the other.

Now, there wasn't a man on the base who could countermand a general's orders. However, wives were a different story altogether. After a short, what I presumed to be "pressured" conversation with the wives, the generals surprisingly decided that perhaps indeed the theater detail would need a better venue. Beyond all my hopes and expectations, we ended up being assigned to use the brand new Service Club with proscenium stage to entertain the troops. And that's how the Ladd Air Force Base theater was born.

The service club was a fantastic facility. And strangely enough, when word of our little theater got out, a fleet of young, aspiring thespians came out of the woodwork . . . female thespians . . . actresses. Ah, yes, the perks of being a producer/director were becoming more evident.

In the remaining seventeen months of my time defending our country from polar bears and wayward penguins, we did a production a month, doing nearly every aspect of each show ourselves. And that was the way we wanted it. You see, any time we were involved with a production, we were excused from active duty. And we made sure we were "involved" a lot.

It turned out that the shows didn't quite take up all of my soldiering time, so I got myself a job. Taking on alternative employment while on active duty was against the rules, but I couldn't be bothered with such claptrap. Keeping in mind my MOS, which is army talk for your job, I began working at a local music store about a mile from camp. There I was able to order classic plays on vinyl from England which really helped our theater group. As you may be sensing, I didn't do a whole lot of real soldiering.

Being as I was stationed in Fairbanks, I rarely went outside. "Cold" doesn't even begin to describe it. I was a nondrinker in those days, not through any righteous convictions, but more so that I just hadn't found any kind of alcohol that I really liked. Near the end of my tour, however, David and Dick decided they wanted to achieve the impossible: to get me loaded. So they held the first and only "Get Peter Brown Drunk" party.

Now, I'm nothing if not agreeable, so I was O.K. with what they wanted to do. After all, I was pretty sure they couldn't get me drunk.

Shows what I knew.

That night, they continuously offered me a wide array of drinks, always saying, "Try this, try that." I'd barely get one drink down before another one was in my hand. My feelings of alcohol non-susceptibility soon flew out the window about the time I flew out the front door. I was somewhere between needing fresh air and searching for a place to hurl. I was very drunk.

I stumbled outside and the fresh air, the twenty-degrees-below-zero fresh air, slapped me upside my head. I dropped like a bag of wet doorknobs. The guys came outside laughing and dutifully dragged me back into the house. That was on a Saturday night. When I finally felt better, it wasn't Sunday; it was Monday. My two-day hangover became the stuff of what legends are made, at least at the Ladd Air Force Base.

The army and I parted amicably enough in June of 1956. In those days, you could get out of the service three months early if you could establish that you were going on to college. I let them know that I had enrolled at the Leland Powers School of Radio, Television and Theatre in Boston.

They said, in essence, "Don't let the door hit you in the ass on your way out!"

I was shipped back to the states. Remember, Alaska was still a territory at the time (Can I really be that old?) I got to Seattle where I made a side trip to buy a 1941 Pontiac. Boy, I was hot stuff then.

From there, I drove on down the coast to Fort Ord to be discharged. I had it all going for me now. As I drove along the shoreline towards L.A., I thought, *Ah, to be young and carefree and have the army willing to pay for your education.*

My before-stated plan was to go to acting school in Boston with David. But there was a three-month "Film Studies" course being taught in the Theatre Arts Department at UCLA by the respected film professor, Ralph Frood, and since I knew I was going to be in the movies someday, attending film school to learn "film acting" seemed like a great idea. I figured that after those three months, then we'd head to Boston. God must have a good laugh when people make lifelong plans, especially at my tender age.

I took an apartment in a dorm at UCLA and picked up a job at the famous Will Wright's Ice Cream Parlor in Westwood. My exposure to the L.A. lifestyle and celebrity came fast. On my second day on the job, who should come in to the shop but none other than the gorgeous Doris Day. She was trying somewhat to hide her identity behind sunglasses and a scarf, but she wasn't succeeding. It was her.

Doris scanned our selection of ice cream, then ordered a hot fudge sundae. I scurried around the kitchen like a squirrel storing nuts for the winter. Never being one to do anything half-ass, I overloaded the sundae, piling on the hot fudge and whipped cream, the nuts and two cherries. I proudly presented it to her as if I was offering a sacrifice at an altar.

At that moment, a funny thing happened. Doris reached into her purse, fumbled around a bit, and then looked up at me, obviously quite embarrassed.

"I . . . I don't seem to have any money," she said.

She could have said, "I don't have any clothes on" and it wouldn't have mattered to me. I was transfixed by her beauty.

"I don't have any money," she repeated. "I'm so sorry."

Ah, Sir Galahad to the rescue.

"No problem," I said. "It's on me."

And with that, I comped Doris Day for one hot fudge sundae. She coyly smiled at me as she picked up her giant ice cream concoction, then gave me a sly, little wink.

"I'll get you next time," she said and walked out of the store ... and my life.

I never saw her again . . . or the money for the hot fudge sundae.

In class, Professor Frood had heard me talking about my career plans in Boston. He, however, was a definite west-coaster, so he began massaging my ego while earnestly attempting to talk me out of making that move.

"You have the talent, the looks, and the drive to warrant staying on in Los Angeles," he said. "Try your luck here in films. Give this town one year . . ." He paused for dramatic effect. ". . . and I guarantee you'll never leave."

He had me at "talent, looks and drive."

The professor had recruited Jeff Corey as an acting teacher. He recommended I take a "film acting" class from Jeff; it was really quite different from stage acting.

Jeff Corey was an interesting guy. During the McCarthy-era Red Scare, Jeff had been blacklisted even though he was a military veteran. He had used the GI Bill to study speech therapy at UCLA. A fellow student asked Jeff to organize a class in speech. Soon, he was teaching out of the garage of his Hollywood Hills home. The students flocked to him. He added to his curriculum and expanded his garage to create a small theater where his students performed scenes. It was into this unusual educational setting that I walked.

In the garage, Jeff had erected risers where a myriad of aspiring actors would sit. On my first visit, I met the very young Jack Nicholson and Sally Kellerman. Nicholson took a quick liking to me.

"Brown," he said in that now-famous Nicholson twang, "I like being in class with you. We all have the questions, but you have the mouth."

I liked Jack and I really liked Jeff's course. It was very hands-on. We were always doing any of a number of different types of scenes with any of a number of different types of actors. I absorbed it all like a ravenous sponge.

I was also very into Professor Frood's excellent course, so much so that I soon canceled my plans to go to school in Boston with David, much to his chagrin. Instead of taking courses in the exotic locale of Boston, I added additional classes in the garage of Jeff Corey.

With the dorm life not being quite my style, I soon went out and rented a small, affordable apartment on Orange Grove Drive in Hollywood. This was very exciting, my initial night in a committed relationship with the city of my dreams. Unfortunately, things quickly turned around.

The first evening in my new digs started out most innocuously. I was having a glass of wine and reading a play when I got sleepy and went to bed. At 3 a.m., I was awakened by, of all people, my landlord. He was there in my bedroom touching me in a very private spot. Although I was that kind of boy, at least with women, with men? Not so much . . . or more likely, not at all!

Reacting quickly, I leaped to my feet, grabbed my amorous intruder, and threw him through the plaster wall. That gives you an idea of the quality construction of my lavish accommodations.

In a panicked rush, I tossed into a suitcase whatever I could grab of my limited worldly belongings and got the hell out of there. My first experience with a gay man had almost cost my landlord his life. I felt a small pang of guilt, of worry for him, but that soon passed. I wasn't going to let that incident sour me on the city of my dreams.

On the sidewalk at 3 a.m., I calmed down enough to realize I really hadn't thought this thing out.

What now?!

I remembered a girl I knew, Janet Novak, who lived nearby, so I called her and asked for temporary asylum. Thankfully, she was agreeable to my hanging out at her place for a few days. The next morning I went back to my apartment to retrieve a few other items. I happened to bump into my ex-landlord; I thought he was going to shit his pants, so fearful was he of another attack. I held up my hands to indicate that wouldn't be the case.

"I didn't appreciate last night, but I'm moving on. I'll get out of your hair, but I want my deposit back . . . NOW!"

With some walking-around money in my pocket, I was soon able to get another apartment. This one was on Sunset Boulevard. I thanked Janet for her hospitality. It turned out that we became great friends and still are to this day.

Now, I began looking for work, real work, in my chosen field. Ironically, the first job I got was doing a commercial for . . . wait for it . . . the army.

Yes, after just getting out of a two-year hitch in the the armed services, there I was asking kids to join the army and see the world. Deep down, I wasn't real comfortable doing it, but it was a job, my first paying job on the fringes of the business, and it headed me in the direction of getting that all-important SAG card.

The SAG card (Screen Actors' Guild) is crucial for any actor who wants to be working in L.A. Getting the coveted SAG card would make it easier to get an agent, go out on interviews, and impress women at bars. To qualify for SAG, you had to work for a production that was signatory with the Guild, "signatory" meaning a formality that a producer goes through to identify the rate of pay. The trick was, these production companies usually wouldn't hire you if you didn't have the card, and you couldn't get the card unless you worked for one of these companies. A real "Catch 22."

Somewhere along the line, you'd have to catch a break and get a contract that was already signatory. You'd first get the job with the appropriate company, then go to the Guild and show them your schedule and tell them you wished to be part of their organization. Once those hoops were all jumped through, they'd welcome you with open arms, especially when you paid the substantial members' fee.

In October of 1956, I climbed the mountain . . . I got my SAG card. I was member 00007686, a number that suits my personality, don't you think? Getting that card meant that I now had to be paid the Guild's union wages, and that I could not work for any company that was not signatory to the Guild. My qualifying performance for them had been my appearance in the Warner Bros./Jack Webb/ Defense Department propaganda film *Red Nightmare*, later known more familiarly as *The Commies Are Coming, The Commies Are Coming*. I say "propaganda" because, basically, it was a recruiting film to get guys to join the army. I was starting to see a trend here.

Things really started picking up for me then. In short order, I acquired my AFTRA card (American Federation of Television and Radio Artists), another union, and then after just a few auditions, got parts in several plays at local theaters. I was offered a job at the Horseshoe Stage Theater understudying the lead and stage managing *Desire Under the Elms* by Eugene O'Neill. I accepted both positions mainly because the leading man was Corey Allen who had just finished the movie *Rebel Without a Cause* with James Dean. I loved his work and knew that I would be able to learn a lot from him.

In time, Corey Allen became a great friend of mine. Corey (original name Al Cohen) came from a pretty feisty family; his father, the vice-president of the Sands Hotel and Casino in Las Vegas, had gained a bit of notoriety for being the man who punched Frank Sinatra in the nose after a gambling-credit argument at the Sands. Normally, that would not have been a great career move, but somehow, it worked itself out.

became a legendary director later in life, but in his early years, he was quite the actor. He also did one of the nicest things anyone has ever done for me: he didn't show up for a performance.

Now it was better than it sounds. As I said before, in addition to stage-managing *Desire Under the Elms*, I was also understudying Corey. One night, he came up to me and said, "Peter, a week from Friday, I'm going to be sick." He smiled conspiratorially.

I looked at him with an eye askance. *How the hell does he know he's going to be sick a week from Friday?* I naively thought.

"I will be sick," he added, then gave me a wink. Winking seemed to be a pretty popular means of communication in L.A. in those days.

"You know, you really deserve to play the lead . . . at least once. So call your agent, call your friends, call anybody you know in the business. Invite your people. Tell them to be there Friday."

I have people? I thought.

I guess I did. I got on the phone and called everyone I knew in the city.

Sure enough, the next Friday came, Corey called in sick, the audience was packed with "my people," and I went on in his place. I was nervous, but excited. When the play was over, I felt I had done as good a job as I could. And the audience, even though it was stacked, seemed to heartily agree. That night, I had my first ever curtain call. That one gesture by Corey helped my career immensely. He was so kind.

The Horseshoe Stage Theater was a small theater. So small, in fact, that the audience members had to actually cross the stage to get to where they'd be sitting. That meant it was crucial for them to all be in their seats when the curtain went up.

Now in addition to stage managing, I was also charged with keeping an eye on the ticket booth. On one particularly rainy night, the first act had already started when a middle-aged couple arrived. Unfortunately for them, I couldn't let them in the theater without disrupting the show.

They were quite a pair. The lady walked glacially slow with a cane. Her husband spewed and sputtered and tried to boss me around. All I could do was put them in the ticket booth to get them out of the rain and keep them dry, apologizing profusely while remaining firm that they couldn't go into the theater until there was a scene break. At that time, I'd then show them their seats. They were not happy campers.

After the show, theater owner Ralph Beecher pulled me aside.

"Do you know who those people are? The ones you wouldn't allow in the theater?"

I shook my head.

"That was Albert McLeery and wife . . . the Albert McLeery? The producer of *NBC Matinee Theatre*? Well, you can just cross doing that show off your career list."

I blinked once, twice. Then it hit me: *I have just alienated one of the biggest big shots in Hollywood!*

So much for this aspiring actor's career.

The next day, however, the fallout from the incident did a 180. Apparently, Ralph Beecher could be wrong. Mr. McLeery called and, instead of reaming me out some more, actually apologized for his behavior the previous night. I was speechless.

He went on to say how impressed he was with a young man who wasn't going to let anything mar the integrity of the show, even if it meant pissing off one crabby old couple. He alluded as to how there weren't many people in Hollywood who would have stood up to him that way. Of course, if I had known who he was at the time . . . well, I probably would have done the same thing, but I know I would have felt much worse about it.

Then to put icing on the cake, he surprised me with an offer to come in and read for a role on his show, *NBC Matinee Theatre*. I eagerly went to the audition was oh-so pleasantly surprised when he offered me a role . . . four roles, actually, on four different productions. Stunned, I just managed to eke out a "Thank you."

This was, I felt, my first real paying professional actor job. I was going to be on national TV . . . at least as national as you could be in the mid '50s. Getting a role on *NBC Matinee Theatre* was huge! People have often asked me if my time on the show was exciting, was it a good job? My standard reply then and to this day was and is, "When you're an actor, any job is a good job."

NBC Matinee Theatre was a ninety-minute show, and it was the only live production on TV at the time. All I remember about my first performance was that it starred Isabel Jewell, an elderly woman who was an excellent actress. During the show, and remember again that it was a live show, Isabel's necklace broke. Beads spilled all over the stage, their little rattling noises echoing for what seemed like eons. Ever the professional, she went right on with her dialogue. It was the only time I did a show where I spent an entire scene picking up beads while acting.

I was still a bit of a straight arrow then, but it served me well at the beginning of my career. I didn't go out at night, wanting to always to be able to give my best the next day at work. In this way, I honored the profession and remained true to Pop's work ethic. And it often gave me a leg up against other actors with whom I was competing for a specific role.

The pay for *NBC Matinee Theatre* was O.K., but it was not really enough to live on, so once again I went out to find part-time work. And that's when I took the job at the 76 gas station on Sunset Boulevard. And as you remember from Chapter One, that was the real beginning of my show business career.

"Courage is being scared to death . . .
but saddling up anyway."
— John Wayne —

Chapter 3
Movies

Although television had been very, very good to me, it was the movies where I had long hoped my career would be established. I did have a steady involvement with film, doing over thirty pictures in thirty-seven years, which is a lot considering that my almost constant work on television westerns and soaps from 1958 to 1992 limited the amount of time I was available for the movie studios. While my efforts on film never quite reached the heights which I had hoped, I did do a lot of good work with many great people and experienced much. I wouldn't trade a moment of it for anything.

My first exposure and participation in a full-length movie was in 1957 shortly after I was signed on as a contract player with Warner Brothers, apparently on the strength of my screen test. I did a small, walk-on part in *Sayonara* with Marlon Brando and Ricardo Montalban. Brando played a military man who goes against his principles by falling in love with a Japanese woman during the occupation after World War II. I, along with another young actor by the name of Dennis Hopper, had parts as army MPs. I guess my time in the service was paying off once again. The movie also used the incredibly funny Red Buttons and the ever smooth James Garner.

The next year just before *Lawman*, I landed a very nice role in the Warner Brothers' picture *Darby's Rangers*. This was a true story about the organization of the U.S. Army's first Ranger Battalion during World War II. Once again, I was in a movie with James Garner. This was his first starring role. The cast was very strong; it included Stuart Whitman, Jack Warden, Edd Byrnes, and my old friend Corey Allen. He seemed to have recovered after his *Desire Under the Elms* sickness.

I played "Corporal Rollo Burns" with Venetia Stevenson as my love interest. It was so exciting to have a nice role and to be in a "big-time" movie, even though the scenes of us in Scotland were actually shot on the Warners' back lot . . . come to think of it, everything was shot on the Warners' back lot. Got to watch those pennies.

Darby's Rangers was where I became good friends with Jim Garner. I really got to know and learn from him both on and off the set.

For the next four years, my time on *Lawman* prohibited me from doing much in the area of cinema what with our thirty-nine-week annual shooting schedule. But I was dedicated to maintaining a steady presence in television and films, so when *Lawman* began wrapping up, I was determined to still stay in front of the cameras.

Besides westerns, the other most popular cinematic genre of the day were war pictures. For the second time, I was cast in a true World War II story, the well received *Merrill's Marauders*. On this occasion, we did not shoot on the back lot at Warners'. To do *Merrill's Marauders*, I had to travel halfway around the world for my profession.

Merrill's Marauders was shot in the Philippines. This was so exciting for me, my first time overseas. We were housed at the Clark Air Base just outside Manila. The movie starred Jeff Chandler and Ty Hardin; because of my successful stint on *Lawman*, I was given third billing cast as the reckless sharpshooter "Bullseye." Unlike all the other soldiers in the movie, my character didn't wear a helmet. I've often had that commented upon by military types, saying there was no way a soldier would be allowed out in combat without his "steel pot." My response has always been that it was my choice, that I thought it went with what my character would do.

Go ahead I figured. If I get shot in the head, so be it.

Jeff Chandler was a lovely man and very caring. To show you the kind of guy he was, when my pal Sammy Davis Jr. was in that accident and had lost one eye, he was in danger of also losing the other one. Jeff, a severe accident survivor himself, stepped up and offered Sammy one of his eyes if need be.

On a lesser scale, Jeff did something for me which I'll never forget. We were housed at a BOQ (Bachelors Office Headquarters) which was really just a fancy term for an old army Quonset hut. Will Hutchins and I were roommates on one side of the building; Jeff had the entire other half to himself. The sides were connected by a bathroom.

Now Will and I were both huge Los Angeles Dodgers baseball fans. Unfortunately, neither of us had the foresight to bring a radio along with us on our foray into the Far East. After hearing me bemoaning my lack of contact with the stadium at Chavez Ravine, Jeff thought for a moment, then left the room before returning shortly.

"Here's your games," he said as he tossed something at me.

I grabbed at the object. It turned out to be a transistor radio that looked like a baseball. It was perfect. Will and I beamed, not believing our good fortune. From then on, we were able to keep up with the Dodgers on the Armed Forces Radio Network.

Jeff was a great actor. In the 1950 western *Broken Arrow*, he was the first Academy Award nominee so honored for playing an American Indian. Unfortunately, *Merrill's Marauders* turned out to be Jeff's last movie. And the reason behind the end of a great career was not a pretty one.

One of our pastimes when not on the set in the Philippines was playing softball; there was a game going almost all the time, usually with U.S. Army Special Forces soldiers who were acting as extras. During one game late in the shoot, Jeff hurt his back badly. He was definitely in pain. Since all of his speaking parts were done, I suggested he should just leave, go home and take care of himself. I was sure they could get someone else to do his long shots. Of course, what did I know? Or better yet, who was going to listen to me?

Sam Fuller, our little pissant of a director, said no. Fuller had a bit of the Napoleon complex, a small man who liked to walk around wearing a pistol on his hip. He wasn't about to have his authority undermined in the least, even at the expense of his star's health.

Ever the trouper, Jeff stayed to the bitter end and finished the movie. He did not look good the last time I saw him. Jeff flew back to the States and went right into the hospital. He never got out of there. A botched back surgery resulted in a damaged artery and hemorrhage. In two operations, he received over seventy-five pints of blood, but it was of no avail. He died at the tender age of forty-two. It may not be provable, but deep down I still hold Sam Fuller responsible for the death of Jeff Chandler.

In 1963, not having anything in the hopper for me, Warners traded me to Disney for an actor-to-be-named-later. (OK, I'm just kidding about that last part.) Truthfully, they lent me to Disney to do two movies: *Summer Magic* with Hayley Mills and Burl Ives; and *A Tiger Walks* with Sabu and Brian Keith.

I loved working at Disney. They did everything there first-class. For example, on my initial drive to the studio when I was supposed to appear for a simple wardrobe fitting, the cop at the front gate, much to my surprise, smiled as if we were old friends.

"Good morning, Mr. Brown," he beamed without even checking his clipboard. "Go right on in."

As I soon found out, Disney demanded that things be right. They really did their homework there. My dressing room was accordingly replete with everything I liked to eat and drink (They even had a bottle of rum, my favorite, in my room.) They had decorated the walls and my dressing table with photographs of my family and previous work friends. Nice touches!

The commissary at Disney was especially actor-friendly. They even served liquor. It was the only studio in Burbank that did that. It was well known, however, that you had better not abuse their largesse. They were fair at Disney, but they weren't stupid.

In *Summer Magic*, I played "Tom Hamilton," a rich and mysterious owner of the house into which Hayley's character's family moves. By the end of the movie, she falls in love with him.

Hayley was only sixteen-years-old, so the hours she could work were limited. I had a scene, my final one with her, at a barn dance. As it happened, it was to be shot at the end of a long day. Too long, I guess. The teacher charged with overseeing Hayley's workload decided the underaged girl's time was up, so she pulled her off the set. There was just the one shot left, but to this gal, rules were rules.

Improvising, the director had an extra, some guy, read Hayley's lines. I immediately objected. I felt that to do the best possible job, I needed to act and react to the actual person in the scene, not some way-too-masculine substitute.

"I'm either doing this scene with Hayley or I'm not doing it," I said in my best diva-like voice. It may have seemed petty to some of the less dedicated actors and technicians on the set, but I had to be true to my calling.

The director, James Neilson, ordered a halt to the production and said he'd have a talk with Mr. Disney himself. He made the call. After a short discussion, James handed the phone to me.

"What seems to be the problem?" Walt asked.

"They want me to do an important scene with Hayley but without Hayley," I explained.

Well, at least it sounded right to me.

"OK," he said matter-of-factly, "I'll be right down."

Soon enough, the father of Mickey Mouse and the godfather of amusement parks everywhere arrived. He was wearing a powder blue cardigan sweater, not the power suit I expected from him.

Walt sat there with the director and me and listened thoughtfully to our concerns. After hearing the pros and cons, he said that he'd really like to get the shot now so that the set could be struck. Even the great Walt Disney was not averse to saving a little money. I still opined that it would not be our best shot without Hayley present. Finally, and in a non-threatening way, Walt gave his answer.

"Peter," he said, "we'll try it with the stand-in and . . . "

I groaned. He held up a finger.

"And . . . then we'll look at it tomorrow, you and I. If you honestly don't like it, then we'll re-shoot it with Hayley. Trust me."

That was all I wanted. I knew he was a man of his word. And as I also found out, he was also a man who knew movies and camerawork. When we viewed our jerry-rigged scene the next day, it was fine. I actually liked it.

"Print it," I said to Walt. We shook hands, no harm done, and then he was off to put out other fires.

I loved working with both Hayley and Burl. She was this young, effervescent ball of fire and he was an even-keeled, very knowledgeable actor from whom I would learn even more.

Our English girl Hayley had come with her parents to America and our set. Her father, John Mills, was an accomplished actor who would go on to win an Oscar in 1971 for his supporting role in *Ryan's Daughter*. Mother Mary was a superb actress who had given up the stage to be a playwright and novelist, the better to keep her family together.

My favorite memory of the Mills family was when I took them to see the Los Angeles Dodgers. John Mills had never seen a baseball game, so I took him and his family, including his other daughter Juliette, on an outing to Dodger Stadium. Dean Martin had loaned his dugout box to me, so we had wonderful seats.

During the game, Dodger great Maury Wills got a base hit. He then proceeded to steal second as he so typically did. Only this steal marked the breaking of baseball legend Ty Cobb's long held record for stolen bases in a season. It was very exciting. A member of the L.A. grounds crew came out onto the field, pried second base out of the ground, and awarded the record breaking base to Wills.

I had forgotten how little John knew about baseball; the whole event had made perfect sense to me. But on the way home, John finally had to know.

"Peter," he said, "what was all that nonsense about with Mr. Wills?"

"Oh, you mean when he stole second base?"

"No, no, no," he protested in all seriousness, "he didn't steal it at all; the gentleman in the little blue cap gave it to him."

After catching my breath from laughing so hard, it then took me ten minutes to explain what happened to the befuddled Englishman. And that wasn't even the best laugh we had on that drive home.

The Mills family liked to play a name game where they would guess at movie stars' real names. John started it by asking if anyone knew who "Archibald Leach" was. Mary guessed Cary Grant correctly. Juliette offered the name "Roy Fitzgerald." That one was a real stumper. No one knew that had been Rock Hudson's name. I was getting into the game, so I came up with "Marion Morrison." It fooled the ladies, but John, knowing my cowboy background, correctly surmised I was thinking of the Duke, John Wayne. Finally, Mary spoke up, throwing the original name of Diana Dors, an English actress, at us.

"Who is 'Diana Mary Fluck'?" she asked.

The car went silent for a moment. From the back seat came an eruption of laughter.

Peter Brown with Hayley Mills in *Summer Magic*.

"Moth-errr!" exclaimed a giggling Juliette.

The impish Hayley chimed in.

"Daddy, is that anything like 'fluck off?'"

The staid Englishman slowly turned to the inhabitants of the rear of the car.

"Oh . . . fluck off, Hayley."

With his proper English accent, it was even funnier. We laughed about that one the rest of the way home.

There was more excitement afoot at Disney when I stayed on to do my next film, *A Tiger Walks*, with Brian Keith, Vera Miles, and Sabu. This movie combined Disney's love of both children and animals in a story about a young girl trying to prevent the shooting of an escaped circus tiger. And the reality of this movie was brought oh-so close to home when the tiger we were using in the movie actually did escape. That brought a few nerves to the surface for awhile.

We were shooting on the back lot. The tiger was in a glass cage. The glass had to be completely transparent, so clear that it wouldn't be seen by the camera when establishing shots were being taken. Well, it must not have been seen by the tiger either. Something attracted his attention and, being a cat, he took off after it. The glass, which we thought was safe enough that we really hadn't given the tiger another thought, apparently wasn't that safe. The tiger went through it like it was Saran Wrap.

We immediately scattered in all directions. Fortunately, the tiger was probably more startled than anybody else. There were animal handlers on the set and they got control of him pretty fast. Soon enough, things were back to normal on the Disney set. The tiger was actually well behaved, so much so that two years later he got another gig, this time on the popular science fiction TV show *Star Trek*.

Still biding my time hoping for another western, I was then asked to be in a movie for Columbia where I would be able to use my athleticism. It would be a blast. I was going to be in . . . a surfer movie!

1964's *Ride the Wild Surf* had all the usual beach party movie trimmings of the day: hot girls in bikinis, wild parties at the beach, and surfing, lots of surfing. And, it was going to be shot in Hawaii.

Hawaii!?

I could barely stand it.

We had great, fun people in the cast: Shelley Fabares, Fabian, Barbara Eden, Tab Hunter, and James "Jim" Mitchum, son of legendary actor Robert Mitchum. Fabian, Jim, and I all played surfers. The studio shot a ton of footage of professional surfers at real competitions; they even purchased footage of the Hawaiian World Surfing Championship.

I was very good at establishing relationships. I quickly befriended Jim; we shared a house for the shoot. Boy, he looked just like his dad. Jim was five years younger than me, but we got along famously. We even decided to practice surfing together in LA, but the first toe dipped into the ocean told us otherwise; the water was freezing. So thinking like any young studs might, we naively went to the studio and asked them to merely fly us out to Hawaii a couple of weeks before shooting was to start, then foot the bill for housing so we could practice surfing. Pretty ballsy, huh?

The really amazing part of it was, the producers at the studio didn't bat an eyelash. They took care of it all.

We were sequestered away in a beautiful house on the north shore of Oahu, home to the really serious waves. I mean big waves. Not being total imbeciles, we hired "Rabbit," a fine surfing instructor to make sure we didn't do anything stupid. The studio paid for him as well as a car for us and a per diem. That was the life.

We went out surfing every day for two weeks. Rabbit, Jim, and I worked our way up and down all the beaches. By the time the rest of the cast and crew arrived, we were the pros. It was definitely money (the studio's) well spent.

Fabian was in the movie because he was a box office pull; he had a lot of hit songs and was a teen heart throb to millions of young girls. Unfortunately, the guy was a little stiff; he acted stiffly, spoke stiffly, he even drove stiffly. He couldn't drive a car from here to the wall. He got eight tickets while driving during the shoot. Still, he got the lead, presumably because he was the bigger draw. I've often been asked if I resented not getting the leading character roles when I was clearly the better, more experienced actor. All I could say to that was simply, "You can't fight city hall."

The director decided I should be a blonde so that the three main surfer characters would be more easily distinguished. So they bleached my hair white. And since Barbara Eden was my love interest in the movie, she couldn't also be blonde, her natural color. Her hair became auburn.

Barbara and I became great buddies. We were never more than that; I just wasn't attracted to her that way. I know, I know, you think I'm nuts for not falling in love with *I Dream of Jeannie* Barbara Eden like every other guy in the country. But I was pretty good at being friends with a lot of women.

There was one famous scene where the two of us wrestled. Her character ultimately came out on top with her foot holding me down by firmly pressing against my neck. There was some snickering by the other cast members. I probably let my male ego get the best of me, just for a moment, so when the director called "Cut!" and Barbara relaxed her pose, I flipped over and immediately pounded out a dozen push-ups. I have no idea what I thought I was doing.

The two of us had worked quite a bit on that scene and had agreed ahead of time on how to do it. I was actually the one who taught her how to throw me to the ground. After all, I had to help her make it look like she could take me, ego be damned. It turned out to be a very good scene.

The main problem with the movie was the first director, who shall go unnamed herein. The guy was an absolute mess. The final straw was the food: Fabian, Jim, and I just couldn't eat the box lunches he had ordered. They were crap, almost literally. Somehow the director thought he was saving the budget, but all he was doing was alienating the crew. After all our complaints fell on deaf ears, we finally called the studio. One of the executives came over and to settle the matter, offered to eat a box lunch with us. It only took several bites for a most distressed look to take over his face.

He fired the director on the spot.

You can't have your cast, the ones who are supposed to be bringing in the big bucks, not being treated well. When they fired director number one and then hired Don Taylor as his replacement, everybody cheered. Now we had a movie.

Shooting shut down for a week when directors were being changed. A friend of mine, "Sunny" Sund, the ex-wife of the famous "Don the Beachcomber" bar/restaurant guy, gave me the keys to her condo in Waikiki. I had it all as I regularly moved between the city and the north shore.

Everything about the movie then went well . . . almost everything. There was one scene that was a little dangerous, so much so in fact, that I needed to get drunk to help summon up the necessary courage to complete it.

There was a legend that if there weren't any good waves, one surfer would need to climb all the way to the top of Waimea Falls and then dive in. If a successful dive was made, the legend said that act would raise the surf and create wonderful waves. If a successful dive was not made, then there were rocks at the bottom of the falls with your name on them . . . and probably your face.

Some idiot writer had written this legend into the script. And another of his ilk had decided that "Chase Colton," my character, would be the one to "take a dive." That has meaning in more than one way.

While I was a good swimmer and had been a stunt diver one summer in Washington, I was still not sure about this undertaking (again, more than one meaning). So I climbed up to the top of Waimea and looked down. It was about forty-five feet, but at that moment, I was pretty sure it was triple that. Hence the need for some liquid bravery. Besides, Chase was supposed to be drunk in the scene where he takes the plunge, so I just chalked up my drinking to "method acting."

John Wayne once said, "Courage is being scared to death . . . but saddling up anyway." However, I don't think the Duke ever made a leap like this. Nevertheless, after carefully surveying the situation, I informed the crew that I would do it, but only on my timeline. I was not going until I was ready. Beyond the difficulty of doing the dive while appearing to be drunk, it was extra hard because they had me wearing, of all things, a grass skirt.

Oh yeah, let's make this death defying dive even trickier.

I could have strangled those writers.

When zero hour arrived, I was strangely calm. Wearing my fashionable grass skirt and acting drunk (acting?), I stumbled my way to the top. Looking down, I waited for exactly the right moment. The surf had to be up and the wave needed to be coming in. They fixed two cameras on me, one with a long lens; I thought they should have used five or six. There was no way I was doing this twice. It took me awhile to collect my thoughts and concentrate on my form . . . and also reconsider what I was doing. But it would have been hard on my ego to climb down, not to mention embarrassing. I dove.

And since you're reading this, it's easy to deduce that I made it. No extra takes were necessary . . . or even considered. The rest of the movie was a piece of cake.

My movie career continued on up until about eight years ago, but the roles became smaller, the characters more specific. My television career, first with *Laredo* in 1965 and then with the soaps for the following twenty years, made it difficult for me to commit too heavily to very many cinematic projects. But I still did them, here and there.

I was happy to be able to do the movie *Kitten with a Whip* with my good friend Ann-Margret, although it was not received too well. And once *Laredo* wrapped, I was credited with starring in *Three Guns for Texas* a.k.a. *Backtrack!*, although in actuality, it's being a "movie" was up for debate; it was just a studio compilation of three *Laredo* episodes.

In 1970, two of my movies came out: *Attack at Dawn* was shot in Israel and was about a commando team helping Israeli POWS escape from a notorious Arab prison. I played an American journalist purportedly doing a story on the prison, but actually working as a collaborator in the rescue. It gave me a chance to reunite with the fine actor Rick Jason with whom I had worked on his show *Combat* in the early 60's.

Later that year, I returned to television in a way as I did the TV movie *Hunters Are for Killing.* It was the story of a man coming home from prison to claim his share of his deceased mother's estate while battling his estranged stepfather who holds him responsible for his own son's death. The cast was exceptional: Burt Reynolds, Melvyn Douglas, Suzanne Pleshette, Larry Storch, Martin Balsam, and Don "Red" Barry.

I absolutely adored Suzanne Pleshette. She was married to Texas oil millionaire and professional gambler Tom Gallagher. Years later as a widow, she married the great comedian Tom Poston. Much of the movie was shot in Napa Valley at the Mondavi winery, so Suzanne and I would have lunch right there at the winery almost every day. The great vintner Robert Mondavi took it upon himself to personally serve us lunch.

Burt Reynolds was a very nice guy. A year later, I would work with him on his TV show *Dan August.* I had a great time doing the episode, "The Manufactured Man." The cast was incredible: Mickey Rooney, David Soul, and two young actors who gained some notoriety years later for a little sci-fi movie called *Star Wars*: Harrison Ford and Billy Dee Williams.

Now, as big a star as actors can become in this business, it's still very difficult for them to be totally secure in what they're doing. In *Hunters Are for Killing*, Burt had a scene where he was in a lake and had to paddle out of the water. He immediately came up to me.

"Well, how did it look?" he asked. "Was I all right?"

Now mind you, this guy was a pretty big star and approaching superstardom. The scene he had just done was nothing too big, nothing particularly difficult. And yet he wanted me, a supporting actor, to give him my opinion. It was reassuring to know that even the big names still took their craft seriously.

Another interesting man I met on the set was old-time cowboy actor Don "Red" Barry. Don had been a big . . . no, make that "huge" cowboy hero in the thirties. A little guy, only 5'4", he had nonetheless been a college football star. He achieved his fame when he got the title role in 1940 in the movie serial *The Adventures of Red Ryder*. He was a marvelous actor but had acquired a reputation as being combative on sets and displaying an oversized ego. But when I met Red, he was nothing of the sort. I had no problem getting along with him. In fact, the two of us even went wine shopping together. Unfortunately for Red, I guess he did alienate many casts and crew members. Eventually, his roles got smaller and smaller, the pictures cheaper and cheaper. Finally his career dried up completely. In 1980, he committed suicide by shooting himself. He was sixty-eight.

Trying to branch out in the industry, I turned executive producer in 1973 by starting my own little movie company, Redwine International Films.

Redwine? you might ask.

Yes, "Redwine." During my *Laredo* years, good buddy William Smith had introduced me to red wine. I was not that much of a wine guy before that. But I started to really like drinking a good red wine . . . still do to this day. So when we got together on this movie, the first fun name we came up with was "Redwine." It just stuck.

The first, and unfortunately only movie Redwine made, was *Gentle Savage*, a story about a contemporary Indian out camping who is unjustly accused of murder. It had been written by a friend of mine, Sean McGregor. When I heard about the project, I asked Sean who was producing it. Like many writers, he had not thought that far ahead. So, seeing an opportunity, I told Sean I'd do it.

What was I thinking?

Well, me being me, I jumped in with both feet. Now I ask you, what do you think is the main thing any film needs in order to be made?

Reader: A good story?

Me: Nooo.

Reader: Wonderful actors?

Me: Not exactly.

Reader: An ace director?

Me: Oh, you're such a child. No, the main thing that any film needs in order to be made is . . . (drum roll, please!) . . . MONEY!!

Yes, we needed financing, so off I went to Union Bank with our crude budget and announced to the "nice" man there that we needed $2.5 million dollars. He gulped once, checked the paperwork, consulted his boss, and then came back and offered us a fraction of what we needed. That was not totally unexpected.

Ever the resourceful young producer, I then went to less standard procedures to secure our money. Bill Hayes and wife Susan Seaforth Hayes, good friends from *Days of Our Lives*, put me in touch with a newspaperman from Chicago who put up some money for *Gentle Savage*. I also had a friend who ran a card club on the second floor of a casino in Compton. This guy had money . . . BIG money. Armed with a letter from my bank, I laid out our entire production plan. He nodded every so often but asked few questions. When I was done, he told me to wait, then left the room. So I sat in his office while my then-wife Yvette was down below in the casino spending our hard-earned money doing pulls on the one-armed bandit. After one hour my friend returned and handed me a paper bag. I peered inside and all I could see was cash, a lot of cash. We sealed the deal with a handshake and just like that, our movie was going to get made.

I was doing the afternoon soap *Days of Our Lives* at the time, but I made sure to keep an eye on the progress of the movie. And the more I saw what was going on, the less I liked. It was Sean; as a writer, he was excellent, but as a director, hmmm, not so much. I did not like what he was doing. Even though he was a good friend of mine, business was business. I proceeded to do what any good producer must in such a dire circumstance.

I fired him.

Knowing deep down that no director was going to be able to bring my vision for the movie to the big screen, I then did another crazy thing.

I hired myself to direct it.

Although I was doing my soap gig at the time, I didn't work every single day, so I was able to direct the movie a couple of days a week. And I could also do a lot of my producer duties right from the *Days of Our Lives'* set. I must point out that two groups from whom I got a lot of help saved me on my maiden voyage as a director: 1) my crew, especially the stunt men; and 2) the cast.

Our cast was pretty strong . . . very strong I should say. We had as the star one of my closest friends and *Laredo* cohort, William Smith, playing "Camper John Allen." William also helped produce it. He is such a talented guy. You might think he's nothing more than his muscle-man show business image, but of course, you'd be wrong. Nothing is farther from the man himself than that. Bill took classes at the Sorbonne, the famous university in Paris. Totally fluent in French, he even went on to teach the language back here in the States. Appropriately, he ended up marrying a French girl with whom he had a son. He is one special guy.

We also had the immensely talented Barbara Luna. A wonderful actress with a work bio longer than your arm, she also has such a kind heart. To this day, she's very involved in Hollywood charities. In *Gentle Savage*, she played William Smith's wife. We also had R.G. Armstrong as the bar owner and the highly skilled Gene Evans as one of the cops. Earlier in his career, Evans had even been chosen over John Wayne for a role in the World War II drama, *The Steel Helmet*. But the real coup for our plucky little production company was getting the inimitable Joe Flynn to play "Chief Deputy Moody."

Joe was a wonderful character actor. Who could ever forget his marvelous run as the pompous, vengeful "Captain Wallace Binghampton" in that favorite sixties television show *McHale's Navy*? Getting him, as so often happens in Hollywood, was total happenstance. I walked into the Cock and Bull Restaurant one day and there, sitting alone at a table, was Joe Flynn. It immediately dawned on me: *That's the guy! That's the guy I want for Chief Deputy Moody!*

I just happened to have a script in my car, so I asked Joe if he would be interested in reading *Gentle Savage*. Even as I was saying it, I was thinking, This is such a cliché.

To my delight, he agreed to take a look. And to take my delight up a notch, I got a call from Joe that evening.

"Peter," he started out, "I just have to say this about your script." There was a very pregnant pause. "I absolutely love it! If you let anyone else play my role, I will fucking kill you."

That made it easy enough.

The production went very well. My only real moment of panic was the shooting of our biggest scene. I had bought a half dozen older trucks that only needed to last twenty-four hours. We were going to blow up a tower and the trucks would, for the most part, be destroyed along with the tower. I had gotten the requisite permit to shoot out where my family lived. It was open country back then. For everything that was involved, we really had to do it right and we had to do it in one take.

And we did.

Only . . . the next day I couldn't find the shot on the film. I looked everywhere. We had crew and cast turning the place upside down looking for it. As it so often happens, I finally found it in the last place I looked (old joke, I know). It was on the "B-roll," the alternate, backup footage used to splice into the main shots. It's where I should have looked in the first place.

Other than that little snafu, everything went swimmingly. I actually got it done on time and within the budget. Go figure.

Gentle Savage was released in March of 1973. I still remember the tag line used to promote the movie:

This DEFINITELY wasn't Camper John's day.

Ultimately, I took our movie to the Santa Monica Film Festival where I was able to sell it. It was really kind of a horse trade there. Although we didn't make a fortune, everybody did get their money including the bank and my backers. And we did end up getting the rights to distribute internationally. I was proud of what we accomplished. I was also sure I wasn't going to be doing that again.

Now nearing my forties and being firmly ensconced in the soap opera world, I sought less and less film work. In the following two years, I appeared in three films with some very fine actors. I did the independent *Memory of Us* which we shot at Will Geer's house. And then there was the blaxploitation film *Foxy Brown* with the smart, pretty, and totally voluptuous Pam Grier. I was the bad boy in that movie. With an audience that was eighty percent black, I joked at the premiere, "All I'm asking is that they let me out alive!" And I also did *Sunburst*, a stalker movie with Robert Englund, and this was before he became the infamous "Freddy Krueger."

The movies came calling less and less, but I still enjoyed working them when they did. It was an honor to work with quality actors and actresses such as Rudy Vallee, Elke Sommer, Andy Griffith, Jill St. John, and Jan Michael Vincent, just to name a few. The movie industry was a great business when you were working, but it was a tough business when you're not.

Thankfully, I still had the soaps . . . and many other television opportunities.

"Bob, you have no idea what it's like to be incredibly good looking."
— A memorable comedic line of mine
from The Bob Newhart Show

Chapter 4
TV

As I've said before, "When you're an actor, any job is a good job." And with the cowboy craze fading on television, it looked like I was going to have to spread my wings and try some different kinds of roles. There was good money to be had being a guest star on other television series; I had done a few during my run on *Lawman*, but they were almost exclusively westerns. But when that show ended, I began branching out, taking roles on a variety of shows. And then when *Laredo* came to a close in 1967, for all practical purposes signaling the end of the oater on TV, I really began making the rounds.

I accepted many guest spots on weekly shows as well as parts in made-for-TV-movies and feature films. The process for appearing as a guest star on a television show is a bit involved. It all begins with your agent and I had a good one. It was a bit unusual how we came to be business partners: it began with my buying a house.

It was early in my career when I mentioned to Sammy that I was house-hunting (that would be Sammy Davis Jr.; I figured you'd know who I was talking about).

"Well," he said, "my agent has a house for sale."

I quickly figured that any house belonging to the agent of Sammy Davis Jr. would be one I'd definitely want to see.

My realtor had already shown me quite a few less-than-appealing domiciles, so she was glad to hear it when I told her I had one I wanted to see. We met at Sammy's agent's home at the appointed time. Just off Benedict Canyon in Beverly Hills, it was a lovely little house, "little" being a relative term for the area. As soon as I walked in the front entryway, I was sold.

"This is not a house!" I exclaimed. "This is a home!"

The "home" was located at 2801 Hutton Drive (There's that address thing of mine again.) At closing, I got a chance to meet the owners, Sy Marsh and his lovely wife Molly. I happily lived there for quite a few years.

Soon after buying the house, Sy became my agent. After a few years, I sold the house to talk-show host Tom Snyder, but Sy remained my agent for a long time after that.

Sy Marsh was considered an ostentatious agent who worked for the highly esteemed William Morris Agency. He did indeed have unusual methods: when he first met the actor Charles Grodin at his agency office, Sy spent the entire meeting talking to him while standing on his desk. I have no idea why. That was just Sy being Sy.

I was so lucky to get him as the steward for my career. He was a "super-agent" long before the term became commonplace. Besides Sammy, he represented the likes of Marilyn Monroe, Elvis Presley, and Steve McQueen. Those were some pretty big-time names for me to be associated with.

Sy was very professional, had great connections, and was well liked in the business. And beyond being an incredible asset to my young career, he became a great friend. Both Sy and Molly were very funny; I enjoyed our friendship as much as our business relationship. He was my agent right up until he passed away seven years ago at the age of eighty-six.

Let's get back to the process for appearing as a guest star on a television series. In most cases, Sy would be asked if I was available. Sometimes he would do the asking if he was aware of a role for which I'd be perfect. For roles studios didn't have anyone specific in mind, a description of them would be put on a list and sent out to actor reps and casting agencies; these lists would describe up-coming scripts and what kind of actors were needed for each one. I was always up for roles that needed good-looking, all-American guy types . . . I'm just sayin'.

Producers often specified that they wanted me for a certain part; other times, I had to go in and read for the role. They knew who I was and what I could do, but if they hadn't seen me in a year or so, they wanted to make sure I still had the "look" they wanted, "look" being code for "Has he put on any weight?"

There was some typecasting, but I typecasted well. I mean, this is a business that so often lives by the typecast. At this point in my career, I was being seen more as a villain than as a good-guy. That was fine with me; playing scoundrels gives an actor so many more layers with which to work.

Accepting a role was usually a dual process, especially the lon-ger I was in the business and the bigger my reputation had grown. The producers and directors certainly needed to approve of me as a choice, but I also needed to be onboard with the production as a whole. I would take a look at the script and decide if it was right for me and if it was something I wanted to do. In the end, I had the final say as to whether or not I would take the part. Over the years, I was offered and took a great many good roles, all of which helped me to create an extensive resume.

After negotiations between the production company and my agent were completed and it was established that I would take a role, I would get a start date. Weekly television series' shooting schedules were usually five days, which gave me a lot more breath-ing space than on the soaps. At the time, I really didn't know how good I had it.

The television studios were mostly in the L.A. area. The "call sheet" I would receive in advance would tell me everything I could possibly need to know about the shoot: times; locations (with directions); phone numbers; names of cast members and their characters; tech crew; schedule for wardrobe, hair, and make-up; meals provided; and pay procedures. It would begin with the time I'd need to arrive for makeup, and it always, repeat "always" had a reminder not to be late. There was a lot of money riding on these shows, shows that were going out to a national audience, so production companies wanted no lost time or money because an actor overslept.

The call sheet would list my scenes and what wardrobe would be necessary for each. I'd have some say as to what I would be wearing on a show. I always talked to the wardrobe mistress, and between the two of us, we'd establish what would be right for my character. It was definitely a collaborative process. As in a lot of show business, you don't want to eliminate creative ideas from creative people.

The first thing I'd do then would be to call Western Costume, the biggest supplier in the business. I'd arrange a time to come in for a fitting, usually well in advance of my first rehearsal. After measurements were taken and small touches added to my costumes, the company would then deliver them directly to the studio.

On the first day of shooting, I would be assigned a dressing room. We'd then do a camera rehearsal, location by location. The actors often got together to discuss how to play particular segments. For large scenes, the cast would do a table reading, especially if there were a lot of entrances and exits. The director controls these readings as well as just about everything else. This is his baby, so he's the boss.

These shows did a few rehearsals, not a lot. My scene shoots would depend on locations; each time there's a location change, it costs money, so production companies do all the scenes that are happening at one location at the same time, regardless of their order in the show. For instance, if scene numbers five and thirty are both being shot in a mountain cabin, then they'd be shot one right after the other, no matter how much screen time has elapsed. If extended periods have gone by in the script, costumes and set pieces have to be changed accordingly. There's a continuity person there at all times to make sure everything appears as it should be from scene to scene.

Sometimes I'd be done with a show and then get called back for a retake. Producers are reluctant to let you leave the set even after your part is done; they're paying you for the whole day, so they want you around just in case a scene needs to be done differently. Therefore, there was a lot of downtime on the set. I read a lot; that was also when I started doing crossword puzzles. Even now all these many years later, I still do a crossword puzzle every day. Good habits are hard to break. It also helps me from getting goofy . . . make that "goofier."

Payment for these shows went through Sy. After he took his ten percent and taxes were withheld, I'd get what was left. Hopefully, it would be above union scale. An agent would always try to get you as much money as possible. Besides upping his cut, he'd be trying to build your career, which benefitted both actor and agent in the long run. Only once did Sy have me take a pay cut; it was to work at Disney. When I asked him why, he had a simple answer.

"Because it's Disney."

As I later found out, word spreads like wildfire in this business. If you want Disney to know you're available, just tell someone in the makeup room at Fox. It's dollars to doughnuts then that you'll soon get a call from Disney.

On the soaps, I was usually around long enough that the casts would develop a real family feeling. However, that was definitely not the case when I was appearing as a guest star. You just don't establish the same relationships on those shows. The regulars may have them with each other, but although the actors were always very pleasant, they usually gave me the feeling that I was nothing more than a necessary outsider.

I did so many guest spots over the years that it's very difficult at this stage in my life to remember the specifics of most of them. The main thing I remember is that one week I would be playing a bad guy on a lawyer show, then the next week I was a bad guy on a police show, and then the next week I would probably again be a bad guy, this time on a doctor show. But now, they all kind of run together. Maybe if I had just done movies in that part of my career, I'd be more forthcoming remembering specific projects. Movie casts get that same kind of camaraderie that TV series regulars have. I just went where the money was.

My first non-cowboy role as a guest star was on *Hawaiian Eye* during the summer of 1962. That same month, I did an episode of the hugely popular *77 Sunset Strip* with my good friend at the time Edd "Kookie" Byrnes. I must have done an OK performance, because that winter they brought me back for another episode. It was good I was taking those jobs, because in just four short months, unbeknownst to me, my gravy train, *Lawman*, would be canceled.

In early 1963, I was particularly excited to be cast on *The Alfred Hitchcock Hour* in the episode entitled, "Death of a Cop." Even though the great man himself was there in name only, it was still an honor to be working on anything even remotely associated with him. I worked closely with the lovely Inger Stevens. My character menaced her character most severely. The role was a wonderful stretch for me as I transformed my usual sweet, innocent self, this time as a carefree surfer, into a total nut case who scared the bejesus out of Inger's character. It was quite a learning experience for me, one that helped my young career so much in the area of character development.

Also during that show, I met and worked with a most incredible man, Victor Jory. Our paths would cross many times in our ensuing careers. In this performance, Victor played my father, a role he would reprise again in an episode of *Kraft Suspense Theatre*. Coincidentally, we had each been featured in the same issue (September 3, 1960) of *TV Guide*. Years later, we were even co-grand marshals for the Mardi Gras parade in New Orleans.

Victor was one hell of a man. Born just after the turn of the 20th century up in the hard scrabble Canadian province called the Yukon, Victor learned early on that to make it in life, he had to be tough . . . fair, but tough. As a young man in the military, he became the boxing and wrestling champion of the Coast Guard. Once out of the service, he kept up his burly physique by working as a circus strongman. In 1930, he made his Hollywood debut, going on to make over 150 films in his long and storied career. He's probably most famous for his role as the cruel slave overseer in the epic movie *Gone With the Wind*. Three years after that, he starred in the incredibly popular movie series, *The Shadow*, playing Lamont Cranston. For those of you too young to remember, Lamont Cranston was *The Shadow*. It was a secret identity thing.

My favorite story about Victor shows you what kind of a man he was. Working on a western movie shoot in his early years, no one really knew him or about his background as a circus strongman. Some of the guys from the movie, including John Wayne and Big Boy Williams, were up for a little poker after the day's filming. Victor had been invited to take a chair. The group had been playing quite a while and Victor had done very well for himself. It was getting late, though; Victor reasoned fairly that it was time to turn in, what with tomorrow's call being just after sunrise. He got up and headed to the door.

"Hold it right there," hollered the Duke. "You're not leaving with all of our money!"

"Yeah," bravely added Big Boy. "Sit down!"

That wasn't near enough to stop Victor. He paused for a moment at the door, shook his head, then turned and squatted down, laying all his night's winnings on the floor.

"Here it is, boys," he announced. "If it's that important to you, come and get it."

John Wayne eyed the newcomer warily, waiting for the scene to play itself out. Big Boy, on the other hand, leaped up and greedily went right for the cash.

BAM!

Big Boy never saw it coming. Victor's meaty right fist knocked Big Boy flat on his back. He was out like a light. Victor looked around the room seeing if there was anyone else who wanted a piece of him. The place went silent.

Finally, the Duke chuckled. He leaned back in his chair and said, "Good night, Victor. Sweet dreams."

Later that year, I worked on *The Gallant Men* with Vic Morrow, a man I respected immensely. I still wince when I think about him being killed almost twenty years later during the filming of a Stephen Spielberg produced film, *Twilight Zone: The Movie*. The really weird thing about him dying was that he had always refused to fly in a helicopter, saying he knew one would be the cause of his death. But he wasn't in a helicopter when he was killed . . . one crash-landed on him during a battle scene, thus fulfilling his premonition.

I continued bouncing around TV land for a couple of years. I remember doing a pair of episodes for the *Kraft Suspense Theatre*, then two more cowboy shows: *Wagon Train* and *The Virginian*. But in 1967, I went off-character to do one of the most intense pieces of acting in my career.

I was cast in an episode of *The Danny Thomas Hour*; this was not the Danny Thomas show with Marjorie Lord and the kids, but instead it consisted of a different kind of show each week, including some heavy drama. In the episode titled "The Enemy," I played a German spy who had infiltrated an American squadron. My good friend Sammy Davis Jr., whom I had gotten to know very well when he appeared on *Lawman*, played a key role in the show. His character was the one who finally exposed mine as a spy when he goaded me into calling him "Nigger." Only, as a German spy, I mispronounced the word, calling him "Niger."

"IT'S NIGGER, YOU ASSHOLE!" he screamed back at me.

It was about as intense a situation on a set as I had ever experienced. Just remembering the utterance of that word now makes my skin crawl.

Fortunately, I was able to put it out of my head almost immediately and go on with my character. When I think back, I'm amazed at how I was able to get that anger going in my role, especially when I was using it against a man I loved like a brother.

I had fun doing an episode of the very hip show, *The Mod Squad*. At least I think I had fun. We did the shoot in Malibu, always a great place to be. After the wrap, I drove back to the Paramount Studios to get my stuff. When I got there, I realized all my personal belongings were gone. Then I remembered: I had put my stuff on the trunk of the car after the shoot, forgot it was all there, and then had driven off. Kicking myself the whole way, I raced back to Malibu, positive that it had been scattered to the four winds. But amazingly enough when I got back, it was all there in a pile in the parking lot: my clothes, watch and wallet, all still there. I guess luck was a lady that night.

In 1970, I landed a plum role in an action show called *The Most Deadly Game*. The cast was outstanding: the regulars included George Maharis, Ralph Bellamy, and Yvette Mimieux, while I was joined on the guest squad by Pat Harrington, Billy Dee Williams, Barbara Luna, and Daniel J. Travanti. Barbara and I have remained the best of friends over the years. I talk to her all the time. She's a very social gal, one who has many female friends in the industry. She is one of the organizers of the legendary charity ball, "The S.H.A.R.E. Party," held at the Beverly Hilton Grand Ballroom. Everybody is invited to her party. You go there to be seen, and of course, in doing so, a lot of money is raised for charity.

In 1971, I got into some lighter fare doing a spot on *My Three Sons*. As with so many of these shows, I was continually meeting people who were or would become huge names in the business. On this episode, I played a teacher; one of my students was the then eight-year old Jodie Foster. From what I could tell, she had a bit of a crush on the old teacher. It brings me great joy to see all the success she has achieved.

Another big name I met on this show was Fred De Cordova. He's most famous for being the longtime producer of Johnny Carson's *The Tonight Show*. A lot of people didn't realize it, but back then he was also producing *My Three Sons*.

Speaking of big names, two months later I signed on to do *Dan August*, another action show, this one starring Burt Reynolds. I was a little bit in awe of Burt, but he put me at ease right away.

I also did a *Mission Impossible* in 1971. It had been a very hot show for five years when they asked me to appear. My character was a sleazy, vicious hoodlum named . . . now get this: Johnny Brown. The writers must have been a little tired when they came up with that one. Anyway, my character was on-screen a lot.

I didn't do many comedies for reasons only heaven knows.

Hey! I'm a funny guy!

The funniest comedy I ever appeared on was *The Bob Newhart Show*. It premiered in 1972, paired up with the dynamite duo of *The Mary Tyler Moore Show* and *The Carol Burnett Show*. In the third episode of its inaugural season, I managed to get off a line that, to this day, still has people reciting it to me five to six times a year.

The episode started out with Bob's secretary rushing in and blurting out, "There is the most gorgeous person out there I have ever seen in my entire life!"

Enter me.

I'm dressed in whites as a tennis pro. I'm there to see psychologist Bob to help me with my personal problems. I get right to the point.

"Bob, you have no idea what it's like to be incredibly good looking."

Bob's show was being filmed in front of a live studio audience, although the editors did utilize a "laugh track" in post-production whenever necessary. It definitely was not necessary here.

The place exploded in laughter, half because of the line and half because of Bob's expression. After about thirty seconds, the audience finally calmed down. With his usual expert timing, Bob offered the next line.

"No. I suppose not."

More huge laughter.

Bob along with Suzanne Pleshette, who played his wife "Emily," were a joy to act with. We all got along very well. Suzanne and I had worked together a few years earlier on a movie, so it was good to reconnect with her.

As my soap opera career sped up, I began doing guest appearances on other shows less frequently. During 1973, I only appeared on one non-soap show; it was *The Magician* with the late, great Bill Bixby. He was such a nice man.

In 1974, I secured work on two episodes of *Police Story*, a realistic cop drama which had lead characters varying from week to week. The first episode starred Angie Dickinson in what basically became the pilot for her eventual show *Police Woman*. Angie and I got along well. When I came back in eight months, the all-star cast included *Star Trek's* William Shatner, *The Walton's* Michael Learned, *Quantum Leap's* Dean Stockwell, *F-Troop's* Larry Storch, and my old mentor and pal, *Lawman's* John Russell. Unfortunately, John and I had no scenes together.

I did like Bill Shatner; in time, we became good friends. I once wrote a script that I wanted Bill to take a look at. I visited him at his office at Universal Studios. After our initial greetings and a bit of catching up, I laid my script on his desk.

"Bill, I'd like you to take a look at something I've written and give me your opinion."

He played with it on his desk awhile, but didn't open it. He hemmed and hawed, then finally came out with it.

"Sorry, Peter, no can do." I stared at him, not knowing what to say. "It's a lawyer thing, you know? The studio is very strict about this. They're afraid if we read an unasked-for submission, it'll come back to bite us in the ass when somebody sues us for plagiarizing their idea. Legally, I just can't do it."

"That's fine, Bill, " I said. "I understand."

We said our good-byes and I headed down the stairs. However, before I had even gotten off the lot, I got a call. It was Shatner.

"I can't do this to my friends. Get that thing back up here," he demanded. "Fuck 'em! I'll read it!"

And he did, giving me some wonderful feedback and a few notes that really helped. Some people you just click with. I clicked with Bill.

My run of working with big name, class actors continued. I did *Marcus Welby* with Robert Young. To my way of thinking, that kind, generous man truly was "Marcus Welby." I liked Jack Klugman during my short stint on his *Quincy M.E.* show, and it was a hoot still doing my own stunts at age forty-three with Lynda Carter on *Wonder Woman*. In that one, I played a schemer who found himself hanging from a rooftop in Studio City. Lynda and I got along terrifically. To put it in a Frank Sinatra type reference, Lynda Carter was "a really good broad."

I loved my time with Karl Malden and a very young Michael Douglas on *The Streets of San Francisco*. Karl Malden was a prince, exceedingly talented, and just a nice, nice man. I especially enjoyed my spare time there in San Francisco; as I've said, my old friend, J.J. Smith, was showing horses at the Cow Palace, so I'd head over there whenever time permitted and help out with exercising his horses.

In 1978, *Charlie's Angels* was in the middle of its incredible five-year run. I'm often asked if I had "hit on" any of the "Angels." They were all such beautiful gals. But I knew that in situations like these, you had to be super-careful not to come on to them in any way. Word spreads fast in this industry, and you definitely didn't want the reputation of being some guy with a proclivity for hitting on young starlets. That's a good way to end your career in a hurry.

Although I wasn't cast in very many comedies, it didn't mean I couldn't have some fun during the more dramatic shows. Later that year in *Vega$*, I had the good fortune of being able to work with Robert Urich and the legendary Tony Curtis. Robert played private detective "Dan Tanna"; incidentally, his character was named after the famous restaurant, not the other way around.

In this particular episode, I played a lifeguard trying to help Dan catch a rapist. The script had Dan getting me an undercover position at a dude ranch, but I resisted. My character then announced that horses spook me and that I would never have anything to do with them. And this was all coming from a man whose career originated because of his ability to ride a horse. Sheesh!

Similarly, in Robert Wagner and Stephanie Power's melodramatic *Hart to Hart* back in 1983, I played a soap opera actor who was a doctor on this show-within-a-show. The joke there was, of course, that I had earlier played a soap opera doctor on *One Life to Live* for seven years. My good friend Stephanie recommended me for the role.

I was enthused about acting with Stephanie and Robert. Unfortunately, the writers didn't seem to share my enthusiasm for the project. They didn't take advantage of the situation the way they could have. I think it showed in my performance.

I really enjoyed working on the show, however. Robert Wagner is a prince, that's all I can say about him. And it was fun being with Stephanie Powers again; the two of us had dated for two years earlier in our careers, so it was great to catch up with her.

Probably the worst experience I had during my days of being a guest star came on the hillbilly comedy, *The Dukes of Hazzard*. Catherine Bach, a sensational lady, was one of the sexiest women I had ever seen. Tom Wopat and John Schneider, the "Duke" boys, were great. But Sonny Shroyer, the fellow who played "Deputy Enos Strunk," well let's just say he came closer to ending my career than any bad role I had ever done.

Now I was pretty good at stage fighting; in both *Lawman* and *Laredo*, I got into my fair share of scrapes with hardly a scratch on me in all those years. I had learned from some of the best stuntmen around how to take a punch and how to make it look like you were connecting when you threw a roundhouse right. But Sonny, that big, dumb ox, had apparently not yet learned his acting craft, especially the art of stage fighting. He was a strong son-of-a-gun. During our fight scene, he was supposed to miss with a punch. But instead, he smashed my jaw, knocking me down. It hurt like hell. The guy almost killed me. I always wanted to even up the score with him. Of course I suppose now, nobody wants to watch two old guys going at it.

A year later, I dealt with the other end of the talent spectrum when I discovered a young actress who I knew had the abilities to go a long way. I was playing an artist, a painter of ladies portraits, on *Fantasy Island*. I was so impressed with one of the young actresses that, while I didn't actually "discover' her, I did predict eventual stardom for her. And that young woman did turn out to be a star: Michelle Pfeiffer.

I then broke into the rarefied air of the prime time soap opera. I made that tremendous leap when the epic show, *Dallas*, came calling.

Just a little over a year earlier, *Dallas* had gone viral on the Nielsen ratings charts with its seminal episode, "Who Shot J.R.?" Viewers had to wait the entire summer plus another two weeks of a Screen Actors' Guild strike to get the answer to the famous question. When that night finally came, everybody, and I mean "everybody" tuned in. Eighty-three million people, an astounding seventy-six percent of that evening's television audience, watched that night, making it, at the time, the highest rated television episode in U.S. history. And now here I was, little old Peter Brown from Long Island, New York, about to appear on the premier show of its time. And the really amazing thing was, I didn't have to read for the role, nor did Sy go seeking it.

They asked for me!

Or at least, their director did. The well-respected Victor French wanted me for a small but pivotal role. It was a scene in a doorway with Linda Gray. So when Sy came and told me Victor French, the Victor French, wanted me for a role on *Dallas*, I said, "If Victor French wants me to do it, I'll do it!" That just goes to show you that one of the things they say about actors is true: We all have egos.

One of my most nerve-wracking experiences in all my years in television occurred in Hawaii in 1982 when I was doing a guest spot on the Tom Selleck star-making vehicle, *Magnum P.I.* We were doing a scene outside in a remote, hilly area when a hurricane-like storm hit the island. In our haste to get the hell out of there, Marcia Strassman, most famously Gabe Kaplan's wife "Julie" on the late seventies comedy show *Welcome Back Kotter*, twisted her ankle. Well, we had one heck of a time trying to get her off the hill. It just didn't look like we were going to be able to get Marcia out of there in time.

Just when things looked their worst, two giant Samoans who had been doing some backstage work on the program showed up. And when I say "giant," I mean it; these guys were huge. They got on either side of Marcia and picked her up like she was a feather and not only carried her down the hill but then also all the way back to the Colony Surf Hotel where we were staying in Waikiki.

The storm had knocked out power to most of the island, so the elevators in the hotel weren't working. And Marcia of course, bless her heart, had the penthouse suite about ten flights up. This additional impediment, however, didn't bother the Samoans in the least. These two guys just began climbing up the stairwell, still carrying Marcia, and got her safely, and what looked like "easily," to her room. I was exhausted, even though all I did was watch.

Simon & Simon, a humorous, light melodrama, was a fun show to do. I appeared on it in 1984 and again in 1986. The co-stars were great guys. Gerald McRaney and I became good pals. He was a big admirer of all things Shakespeare, so after my episode wrapped, I gave him a Shakespeare-related document, although for the life of me, I can't remember exactly what it was.

I also spent time playing racquetball with the show's other co-star, Jameson Parker. I must have beaten him, because for some reason, they subsequently had me wearing a mustache on the show that made me look like a seventies porn star. Payback's a bitch.

I was getting very good at playing the charming villain. Gerald and Jameson soon had me back on *Simon & Simon*, this time trading in the mustache for a white suit. I was, however, still the bad guy, white suit or not.

In 1990, I accomplished the dream of every teenage boy and male college student . . . hell, let's just make that "men of all ages." I had a guest spot on *Baywatch*.

Baywatch had become a cultural phenomenon. The show had achieved a global audience that exceeded one-billion people, an absolutely unbelievable number. Michael Berk, the show's creator and writer of its early episodes, was and still is a good friend of mine. That talented man had originally been a writer on the television show *Manimal* and had scripted quite a few TV movies. He also created, co-produced, and wrote *The Wizard* TV series.

I enjoyed the cast and doing the show, especially since I got sent to a wonderful location for my shoot. My character was in scuba gear for an underwater scene. However, people smarter than me decided they didn't want to shoot it in the ocean, so that meant filming would need to be done in a suitably large aquarium. And the aquarium they chose just happened to be in Hawaii.

Not bad!

In 1992 for just the second time in my career, I was cast in a sitcom. It had been twenty years since I told Bob Newhart that he had no idea what it was like to be incredibly good looking. Well, with a line like that, you'd have thought sitcom directors would have been lining up at the door to avail themselves of my services. As I've said before, "I'm a funny guy."

Apparently, no one was listening.

Wings was the show I was asked to guest star on. It was a very good ensemble comedy, a fun show with a most enjoyable cast. In it, I played a "somewhat" sleazy plastic surgeon, a far cry from my time on *Days of Our Lives* as the noble Dr. Greg Peters. A lot of dramatic actors have trouble fitting into comedies, but I had good comic timing and a nice stage presence. I loved doing that type of show.

My last television guest starring role was at the turn of the century (21st, not 20th, wise guy!) In 2000, I appeared on the military adventure-legal drama, *JAG*. I don't remember much about it. That's funny, because I can remember almost every episode of *Lawman*, and that was more than fifty years ago. It's strange how the mind works.

During my career, I appeared over seventy-five times as a guest star on TV shows from 1957 thru 2000. I have wonderful memories of doing them, met a lot of great people, and wouldn't trade my time on them for anything. But for the most part, they were just 1-shot jobs. The money, although good, wasn't steady and the lifestyle was a bit nomadic. I loved acting but I loved eating too. A steady job in TV was what I really wanted, but after *Laredo*, none seemed to be forthcoming. I wanted security and so for twenty-one years in the middle of my run, I got exactly what I wanted:

Soap operas.

Be careful what you wish for.

"Hey, it's just six weeks and it's a lot of money."
– Agent Sy Marsh to me regarding
my switch to soap opera acting

Chapter 5

The Soaps

I was now thirty-five. My cowboy days on television were pretty much over. Actually, they were pretty much over for everybody, at least that is, everybody but James Arness on *Gunsmoke*. I thought that show would go on forever. As it was, "forever" turned out to be another three years, which made it an even twenty seasons for Marshal Matt Dillon and the gang down at the Long Branch Saloon.

I needed to find something else now, a gig that would keep my acting chops strong and my growling stomach full. So, I did what many of my contemporary Western stars did: I switched from "horse operas" to "soap operas." For the next twenty years, I would "sell soap" on daytime television. And during all those years, I mourned the loss of the great American cowboy on television and in the movies.

It was definitely time to move on. An actor needs to go with the flow, so I made my seismic career change: I entered the depraved world of soap operas.

"Soap operas" originally got their name from the early years of the daytime dramas. These never-ending serials were mostly sponsored by soap companies. Ivory Soap was a big sponsor of *As the World Turns.* Since they were generally on during the day when the viewing audience was predominantly housewives, the demographics dictated that these shows indeed were the perfect vessel for promoting household cleaning products. Thus: Soap Operas.

In 1971, my agent Sy Marsh called and said he had an offer for me to do a soap opera for NBC; the pay would be $1,000 per show for six weeks. That was quite an increase above my initial contract with Warner Brothers fifteen years earlier. Even though a quick tabulation showed I would make $30,000 in a month and a half, I nevertheless stubbornly announced that there was no way in hell I would be caught dead doing a soap. I knew people who did soaps and they hated the rigamarole that went with it. Unfortunately for me, I was idle at the time and anxious for something, anything, to come along. Sy, conscious I'm sure of his ten percent commission, urged me on.

"Hey, it's just six weeks and it's a lot of money."

Six weeks, eh?

I thought seriously about it. Obviously it was a slow time in the industry. Television was much more cyclical then; prime time shows were on for thirty-nine weeks, then off for thirteen during the summer. But soaps were not part of that television pattern. Like death and taxes, they went on forever. I finally caved.

It's just six weeks, I thought. *I can do that standing on my head.*

Now, I have to apologize to my fans of many years for what I am about to write: I am not, nor have I ever been, a big lover of the soaps or of the people who wrote those shows. They just weren't my cup of tea, or at least that's what I thought at the time. I really didn't see myself as a "soap" actor; after all, I was a "cowboy." So, I figured I'd take this little six-week, daytime drama job, knowing full well that something better would be coming along soon.

So much for my ability to tell the future. Remember never to ask for my advice about football point spreads.

Weeks soon turned into months, months turned into years, and finally, years turned into decades . . . two decades to be exact. They had their hook into me and were reeling me in. My six-week gig had become a twenty-year "soap" career on five different daytime dramas.

My first foray into the wonderful world of soap operas was on that venerable favorite of the midmorning set, *Days of Our Lives*. It was the second longest-running scripted television program in the U.S. after *General Hospital*. I should add that *General Hospital* was one of the few soaps on which I did not appear.

Many of the early stories on *Days of Our Lives* were written by Bill Bell. I would come in contact with Bill many times during my soap opera years.

In the seventies, *Days of Our Lives* had the reputation of being the most daring drama on daytime television. They covered topics other soap operas would not dare to do. Staying away from the fluff while delving into serious stuff was a major redeeming factor for me in my quest to do acting that actually mattered. *Days of Our Lives* seemed to offer the best opportunity for me to do quality stage work.

I'm certain I was popular with soap opera producers because I was never the focus of any scandal or vicious gossip. I was very organized, learned all my lines, prepared extensively for each role, and was always on time. What's not to like? I was also not much of a drinker, had no interest in drugs, and was an active sportsman who kept myself in extraordinary physical condition. And beyond that, people in the audience liked me . . . they said I was "cute." I'll leave that up to you, dear reader, to decide.

After *Laredo* ended in 1967, I had made various guest appearances on television series and had been cast in several made-for-TV movies and feature films. Even after I got into the daytime drama business, I continued to take roles in movies and appear as a guest star on nighttime television series.

If I asked you what you thought was the hardest work in the entertainment industry, you might cite being a stuntman or cleaning up after the elephants at the circus or maybe even being Charlie Sheen's publicist. But I doubt any of you would list "soap opera actor" in that category. But as God is my witness, doing daytime drama is just about the hardest work there is in show business. It exhausts me just to think about it.

Soaps are very tough and a huge time constraint. You're on the set for what seems like forever; it's virtually the same as doing a movie every day. For a one-hour show, you'd be lucky if you got the script three days in advance. On *Lawman*, we had three days to shoot a thirty-minute show; on soaps, an hour show was shot in just one day. You do the math. The hardest part was the dialogue; there was just so much of it, especially since there was not a lot of physical action.

An average day on the soaps went like this: I'd get up at 5 a.m. so that I could make it to the studio by 6:30 a.m. for makeup. Once there, I'd receive that day's schedule. Just as we did on prime time television shows, we'd start with a full camera rehearsal for blocking purposes, i.e. a rehearsal of our movements so that everybody would know where to be and where to go during every bit of dialogue. It's amazing the collisions and traffic jams you'd get when even just one actor didn't know his blocking.

We'd do these runs with scripts in hand. There'd be a lot of technical stuff to go over as we always used the three-camera system. During this rehearsal is when I'd tag my cue lines so I'd know when to start talking.

The day's schedule would tell us when the shoot would start. There was little time for retakes, so the pressure was immense to not just know all your lines, but also to not blow any of them when you were speaking. You just dreaded the all-powerful people in the booth coming in over the intercom and saying, "O.K., let's try that one again." That meant somebody had screwed up.

Taping would run late into the afternoon or early evening. When I'd receive my script, I'd pray I wasn't in the last scene of the day, especially on Fridays. If I wasn't in that last scene, I was free to skip out. If I wasn't in the show for awhile, they'd let me know in advance exactly when they would need me. I got paid if I was there or not, no matter how large or small my part was that day.

After that first contract was up, NBC decided they liked my character, so they wanted me to do more. That meant I'd get paid more. I already didn't care much for the work, but I did like the money, and no other great offers were exactly pouring in. Daytime drama paid very well, the contracts being written for so many shows at a certain dollar amount per show. NBC gave me a one-year contract.

It may seem counterintuitive to know that I preferred playing evil characters over good ones, especially after my years as wholesome hero Deputy Johnny McKay on *Lawman*. But you have to know that evil characters are so much more layered than the goodie-two shoes. You can really put your acting chops to work. And financially, it was well known that evil characters seemed to last longer on soaps . . . and thus had a steadier income.

I was always amazed that I, and others like me, managed to last so long in the daytime drama industry. But just like any job that pays well, you get comfortable with all your big-boy toys, you enjoy the fame and the famous people you get to meet, and there's a giant pair of golden handcuffs called a big house in the mountains overlooking Beverly Hills that keeps you locked up and answering your work roll call every Monday morning.

My six-week job went on for just short of eight years on *Days of Our Lives*: 1971 to 1979. I did over 1,000 episodes as Dr. Greg Peters, faithfully showing up every day at the NBC Studios in Burbank. Each year when my contract came around, I'd say "No!" And each year, the salary went up and I'd reconsider.

"Well, I guess so."

I was such a money-whore.

To be credible as Dr. Greg, my prep work was very important, so I took care to learn as much of the language of medicine as I could. We often had a medical ER technical adviser to reference and fall back on. I must have done a good job as a medical man as I many times received letters from viewers asking me in all earnestness for my medical opinions. I guess they thought I was a real doctor who just happened to play one on TV.

"Dear Dr. Peters," one might go. "My husband has an incredibly scaly rash on his hand that extends all the way up to his elbow. He refuses to see a doctor. What would you recommend?"

Well for one thing, I sure wasn't going to shake hands with that guy. I was never sure what to do in these cases and neither was Dr. Greg. And more amazingly, this also happened to me in person. I'd get stopped on the street and asked for a medical opinion. I was so glad that my character wasn't a proctologist.

Regarding the other actors on *Days of Our Lives*, I loved them all and got along with everybody, cast and crew alike. That's hard to believe, but when you're together as much as we were, it's a good idea to get along with each other. We were a team for such a long time that we all became very close.

Macdonald Carey, a great actor whom I respected very much, was the pillar of the show. We all called him "Mac." He voiced the original title sequence which, as far as I know, is still being used today. Mac's iron-man run on the show lasted from 1965 right up until his death in 1994.

Another performer, Frances Reid, played "Alice Horton," Mac's wife. She was on the show from its inception on November 8, 1965, on up until her death on February 3, 2010, a span of forty-five years in which she played the same role. That's incredible dedication.

Another long-timer is pretty Suzanne Rogers who has been on the show for thirty-eight years. And Susan Seaforth Hayes has appeared as "Julie Olson" in all six decades that the show has been on the air. Compared to them, I'm a soap-novice at just twenty years in the business. I am so proud of those gals for all they've accomplished. As of this writing, *Days of Our Lives* has done over 11,700 episodes. It's one of the world's longest running television soaps.

After almost ten years as a half-hour show airing at 2 p.m., *Days of Our Lives* became a one-hour drama on April 21, 1975. Being as focused as I was on my acting, I didn't really notice that much of a difference. It had always been hard work. Now however, the sheer volume of acting was twice as much while still doing the same one-day shoot. Fortunately it was just the same old stuff.

It seemed like there was never enough time for preparation. We were continually getting rewrites at the last minute, often slapdash writing that we didn't respect. It was not how I liked to prepare for a role, but again, I stayed with it for the money. Being "Dr. Greg Peters" was hard work and internally not very rewarding, but the initial contracts were nice. Unfortunately, there were no residuals. My contracts did state that I had the potential to share in foreign profits, but that never happened.

I suppose I'll disappoint my surviving soap opera fans when I tell you I don't have many specific tales about individual shows or actors. I do remember the lovely Bennye Gatteys and how her character, "Susan Martin," married me. At the time, it was a very big deal. Unfortunately, the story lines and episodes run together for me; it's all kind of a blur now.

I did thirty-two *Days of Our Lives* episodes my first year. Fortunately for the show and my career, not to mention my ego, the fan mail came in right away . . . lots of fan mail. Apparently, I was very popular with the ladies. I even had to hire someone to open the mail and sort it. Generally, I sent my fans autographed five by seven photos. Even though it was in the best interest of the show, the studio left it entirely up to me to pay for all the fan correspondence and pictures. Typical.

Things were going as well as could be expected during my *Days of Our Lives* run when I was thunderstruck by a horrible loss. My mom, diagnosed with cancer a while earlier, hadn't been doing too well. Pop was down to taking care of her two days a week; on the other days, my brother Phil and Pop would load her in Phil's station wagon and take her to some far distant hospital for treatment. On one of the days she was at home, a Sunday, Phil stopped by unannounced just to see how she was doing. As he told me, it was the weirdest thing.

"Peter, she was sitting up, she was talking, and then she got up and fixed breakfast," exclaimed Phil. "She just looked so good. We talked about old things. It was like some miracle had occurred. I'll never forget that."

Pop was sitting there with his mouth open, amazed at his wife's recuperative powers. Of course, about an hour-and-a-half later, she got tired and decided to go to bed. Phil said his good-byes, then headed home since he had to be at work the next morning. The moment he came through his front door, he got the call.

Wilhelmina Reaume Brown, our mother, was gone.

She passed away on September 9, 1974. I had been planning to take her to Tijuana for some laetrile treatments, but we never got there due to my work. The woman who had taught me so much, who had given me my start in my life's work, and who had supported me in everything I did, was gone. To this day nearly forty-years later, I still have trouble believing she's not here. I'll love you forever, Mom.

The next show I was on, *The Young and the Restless*, was another venerable television staple, very similar in its longevity to *Days of Our Lives*. *The Young and the Restless* has been on the air for thirty-eight years. Amazingly enough for this present era when soap operas are dropping like flies, both shows have been renewed through 2013 with an option for 2014. That's a credit to the writers for keeping things intriguing and its fans for supporting the shows as long as they have.

The Young and the Restless was created for CBS by Bill Bell and his wife, Lee Phillip Bell. I appeared as attorney "Robert Laurence" in two segments seven years apart: 1981-1982 and then 1989-1991. Shooting took place in an L.A. studio near the Farmers' Market. An improvement I noticed with this show was that the scripts were given to us seven days in advance of the shoot unlike the three that were standard with *Days of Our Lives*. This was a godsend for someone like me who lived for the preparation of my roles.

As I've said before, soap operas are a huge amount of work. The number of lines I needed to memorize for each show was always a lot, but being an attorney in this one with its mountain of dialogue made things incredibly hard, especially for the courtroom cross-examination scenes. I had to paste cue notes all over the set, even on the judge's bench, to help me kick-start my lines. I cleverly placed the small scraps of paper so that I could see them but the camera could not. And I wasn't the only one doing that; the set often looked like an explosion at the Post-it Notes factory.

The use of the word "afraid" isn't quite right, but let's just say we were very wary of making any mistakes. The director would rarely do retakes if the actors screwed up; retakes were generally reserved for when the technicians screwed up.

One actor I got along with famously was Eric Braeden. I'm astonished to know that Eric is still with the show, playing *The Young and the Restless's* charming Victor Newman for the last twenty years. He's known as daytime's most recognizable hero. He's about the only soaps friend I've stayed in touch with over the years.

Eric was a fine tennis player, as was I. The two of us were pretty evenly matched, so we had some epic battles on the court. We traveled together to the many celebrity tennis tournaments that were all the rage at the time. In fact, apart from the show, I spent the majority of my waking hours on the tennis court.

I took my tennis quite seriously. I was good, but I got incrementally better when I began taking lessons from the legendary tennis instructor Pancho Segura. "Segoo," as he was called, had won the NCAA singles title three times during the war and had been the world's number one professional tennis player in the early 50's. He was famous for hitting a devastating two-handed forehand that Jack Kramer called "the single greatest shot ever produced in tennis."

When I worked with him, Segoo was the resident pro at the La Costa Resort in Carlsbad, California. He still lives there today, retired at the age of nintey. My favorite memory of Segoo was when we were partners at a celebrity event against the legendary tennis pro Pancho Gonzales and some woman celebrity. I had broken a string on my racquet, so Segoo gave me one of his. As he was showing it to me, he whispered, "Spin it down the middle," and then nodded at me. At the time, I was serving from the ad court to the great Gonzales.

Now, I was going to be happy if I just got the ball in, but with Segoo's confidence in me, I figured, *What the hell!* As I tossed the ball up, I reared back and gave it everything I had, cutting down hard and twisting the racquet with all my might. To my great surprise, and certainly to Pancho's, I smashed the best serve I ever hit. It whizzed right by him.

"ACE!" hollered the referee.

Pancho had barely moved. I think he had anticipated me hitting the ball to the other side. A look of surprise first registered on his face; then slowly, a smile crept across his lips. I stood silently as I took in the joy of what I had done and would most assuredly never do again. It had been what I imagine it would be like to hit a home run off Nolan Ryan. Although I tried to act like it was no big deal, inside I was jumping up and down. At that moment, I could have retired from tennis and been a happy man.

So anyway, back to *The Young and the Restless.* One incident

Playing tennis in a celebrity event.

that does stand out in my memory had nothing to do with an actual episode. Bill Bell was in his office in Chicago. I was in town doing a movie promo when he called and asked to see me. I assumed it would be one of those social calls where he would want to know what I was up to. But to my great dismay, I walked into his office only to learn that he had heard reports I was showing up late on the set.

Now, anybody who knows me would swear that's something I would never do. I had always prided myself on being punctual and knowing my lines. I wasn't late to anything, especially not to work. Come to think of it, I was early most of the time. Somebody didn't like me (perish the thought!) and had taken to spreading vicious rumors about me. It took a good half-hour to convince Bill otherwise. In the end, he said he figured it had been something straight out of rumor control, but that he needed to hear it from me. Our conversation that day moved on to other things; he was satisfied with what I had to say. It did, however, remind me that this was a cutthroat business and that there were always people out there who would do anything to steal a role or get ahead.

I always felt *The Young and the Restless* was pretty bland. But at least my character got divorced a lot; that way, I could continually be paired with new and more beautiful women. That was the pattern for this character, and in general, for all my characters on soaps.

In 1983-84, I switched coasts for my "art," moving to New York City to appear in a brand new daytime drama called *Loving* on ABC. There I would play "Roger Forbes," erstwhile university president and aspiring politician. That sounds so like me, doesn't it?

The inspiration behind *Loving* was Agnes Nixon who had created the big soap hit *All My Children*. We often referred to it as *All My Kids*. Now, I had been doing daytime drama long enough that

Tennis greats Pancho Gonzales and Pancho Segura with me and my wife, Mary.

I had become a pretty good judge of shows and their characters. And I was absolutely positive that this bird would not fly. At the time, however, I needed the scratch, so I bit my lip and signed on for what I expected to be a limited run. I was not far off.

The way they scheduled me on *Loving*, I only worked a couple of days a week. That was nice. Also nice was the raise I received, besting my salary on *The Young and the Restless* by quite a bit. Truth is, in all my years doing soap operas, I never took a pay cut. Sometimes I'd be paid the same amount from one show to the next, but I never took less. The key for me was staying active.

I took an apartment on the east side. When I came back a few years later to do *One Life to Live*, I took an apartment on the west side. The studio for both shows was just off Central Park West.

At first look, *Loving* appeared to be a strong show. Major social issues were tackled head-on: incest, alcoholism, the Viet Nam War and its resulting post-traumatic stress syndrome. The problem as I saw it was *Loving* suffered from a constant revolving door of writers and producers. As such, there was no continuity to the story lines; the shows never got going and that's what killed it, at least in my inestimable opinion.

There were some pretty strange stories on *Loving*, strange even for the odd world of soap operas. They once went so far as to have a character selling his soul to the Devil. Shades of *Damn Yankees*. It was no wonder then that *Loving* was the lowest rated network soap opera during most of its years. The only reason that ABC stuck with it for as long as they did was due to their faith in Agnes Nixon and the success she previously had with *All My Kids* . . . er, *Children*.

My time on *Loving* was short lived, maybe six months. I was soon written off the show, killed in a "reported" plane crash. They wrote it as a "reported" plane crash in case the producers and directors wanted me to return to the show. But by then, I could see the handwriting on the wall. As we say in the soap business, "You can be shot in the head one day and come back miraculously the next. Who knows?"

I sure didn't.

Although I did not return to that mess called *Loving*, ABC wasn't done with me yet. They simply moved me across the hall to work on another soap. That show was one more longtime mainstay of daytime television, *One Life to Live*. It opened for business in July of 1968 and did not close its TV doors until its final episode in January of 2012. My short tenure as ambassador Charles Sanders lasted only from 1986-87.

One joyous note for me working on *One Life to Live* was the reunion I had with Philip Carey, also known as "Captain Edward

Parmalee" on my cowboy show *Laredo*. Philip was a long time friend, a very fine actor, and, all in all, a good man. He had a wonderful sense of humor even as he was playing ruthless businessman Asa Buchanan for twenty-eight years. A trooper to the end, Phil did his last performance on *One Life to Live* just three months before his death at the age of eight-three.

Phil and I had lunch together almost every day while working in New York, many times with other members of the cast, but often it just being the two of us. Phil was able to drink at lunch without it affecting his performance. He loved his Scotch. I, on the other had, never drank when I was working. I don't think it would have affected me, but I was always so determined to give it my best that I never risked it with alcohol. I guess I just cared too much about my craft.

Marcia Cross was at an early point in her career as an actress when she played "Kate Sanders" on *One Life to Live*. Here was another redhead whom I really liked. My memory is a bit foggy, but I'd be surprised if I didn't hit on her. As you'll be able to tell by the end of this book, I really love the redheads. I was so glad to see that she got the wonderful role of "Bree Van de Kamp" on the hit series *Desperate Housewives*. She's a marvelous actress who deserves all that she has achieved.

My limited time on various soaps was becoming a trend. Soon enough, I was killed off again, only this time it was more of a shock to me. Being written out of a show so permanently is always a difficult row to hoe. On the one hand, you'd think I'd be happy to be let go from one of these shows. But on the other, even though I've stated how little regard I had for this kind of work, I still loved the true art of acting, the creation and maintenance of a good character, no matter what the medium.

Unfortunately, this death was written most cruelly for my character: I got drunk, went to Las Vegas to get married . . . only then to die on my wedding night. How's that for delayed gratification?

I remember my last day on the show. I had been killed off earlier in the week, so my part consisted of me lying dead in Las Vegas in my coffin. And while certainly not trying to toot my own horn, I will tell you that I nailed that scene. Of course, all I had to do was . . . nothing.

I almost fell asleep there in the coffin. That would have been embarrassing, especially if the corpse had begun snoring. On the plus side, it was the easiest money I ever made. Death in soap operas, while being painful because of the job loss, is just the way it goes. At least judging by my fan mail, the public was not happy when I bought the farm. So as Bill Murray said in *Caddyshack* when talking about an unusual tip: "At least I got that going for me."

My last stop on that big bus called "soap operas" landed me back in Los Angeles on CBS's show, *The Bold and the Beautiful*. I lasted there from 1991-92. Once more I was working with Bill Bell who knew me thoroughly from *The Young and the Restless* and *Days of Our Lives*. He had always liked my work, and again, he appreciated that I was always on time. I had to agree with Woody Allen's famous quote: "ninety-percent of life is just showing up."

Bill was the creator and executive producer (EP) of *The Bold and the Beautiful*, and as such, he decided I should be in his show. The EP is the one who creates the story line; it's then the writers' job to flesh out the words. Bill and I got together to decide who my new character should be. Bill suggested the role of a commodities broker, but I told him I would feel better being something more cowboy and less office dweller, more Western and less New York. I finally came up with the brainstorm of being a rich, Texas oil tycoon. That sounds like me, doesn't it?

Bill loved the idea and like that, I was back in the saddle again, so to speak. Meet "Blake Hayes," Texas millionaire oil man.

After a short stint on *The Bold and the Beautiful*, I left the show.

I think they just didn't know what to do with my character. There was no dramatic killing or fatal disease; they just sent me away. As a memento of my last days on a soap opera, I sweet-talked the prop department out of the neon sign from The Starlight Tavern. In the show, The Starlight Tavern was where I met twin sisters both played by Joanna Johnson. An interesting note about Joanna was that after she left *The Bold and the Beautiful*, she went on to create and produce the television show *Hope and Faith* which starred Faith Ford and Kelly Ripa. The show was based on Joanna's life. Strangely enough, Faith Ford played "Hope," not "Faith."

Well, I pray I haven't been too hard on the soap operas. In truth, they were a huge part of my life and kept me going for many years. At the end however, I just wanted to get back to my first love, period Westerns. But unfortunately for me, that just wasn't happening. The closest I came was when I rode in the Rose Bowl parade with the Roy Rogers-Dale Evans Museum group. Dressed in my cowboy finest, I happily trotted my horse down Colorado Boulevard as people began calling out my name. Or at least, I thought it was my name.

"DR. PETERS!"

"ROBERT! ROBERT LAURENCE"

"BLAKE! I LOVE YOU, BLAKE!"

They weren't calling for me or any of my Western characters. They saw me as my soap opera creations, even though I was completely decked out in all my cowboy finest. I put my head down and laughed.

What are you going to do? I thought.

I looked up, broke into a big smile, and waved to all my fans.

*"Do you want to walk with me
down to the horse pen?"*
— My clever come-on to future
(and forever) wife Kerstin Kern

Chapter 6

Women in My Life

Ah, now we come to the wonderful world of love and marriage
. . . two words I've proven don't always go together.

Working in Hollywood had to be the best job in the world, especially if you were a young, attractive TV star. Beautiful women
were everywhere. I was rarely without a girlfriend, and a number
of them qualified for extended-relationship-status.

But I wasn't just a hound dog with the ladies; I loved the idea
of marriage. And I could commit . . . boy, oh boy, could I commit.
Over the course of fifty years, I've committed to marriage five, yes,
count 'em, FIVE times! That's an average of one marriage every 10
years, although only one of them made it that long. I guess I'm still
surprised that the first four ended in divorce, giving me a measly
.200 batting average in the world of nuptials. It's lucky for me that
now I've got a real keeper in Kerstin, or "KK" as I call her, my current wife. It took me a lot of dress rehearsals, but this time I know
I got it right.

Getting married before the age of thirty is just asking for trouble, especially in show business. But back then, I knew it all; I could
handle any situation . . . I thought! With my big-time, glamorous
job at Warner Brothers, I had the world by the tail. So of course,

you'd think I'd really be out there playing the field, at least until my late twenties. You'd think that, wouldn't you?

You'd be wrong.

I met my first wife at the guard gate at Warner Brothers. That should have been my first clue. Actually, it was the guard at the guard gate who introduced me to her. He also happened to be her father.

"You've just got to meet my daughter," he insisted. "You just gotta."

I was a little hesitant to take the word of an obviously biased father, but he was so insistent that I finally agreed. I was so glad I did.

Diane Jergens was a cute, bubbly little thing. And this girl was talented. She was in her first movie at the age of twelve and had later appeared on the big screen with the likes of Spencer Tracy and Gary Cooper. By the time I was introduced to her, she had already performed in popular television shows such as *Dragnet, The Life of Riley, The George Burns and Gracie Allen Show*, and *The People's Choice*. Years later, she was a semi-regular on the renowned *The Adventures of Ozzie and Harriet*. She was almost always the pretty daughter next door.

When we met, she was working on a Warner Brothers film, *The FBI Story*, with Jimmy Stewart. I fell for her and she fell for me, and with all that falling, my head spun so much that before I knew it, we were engaged.

That was pretty heady stuff for a twenty-two-year-old. The fly in the ointment, however, was Warner Brothers: they weren't wild about our relationship. It was better business for them to be able to sell the hot, young, entertainment-farm studs as "single," thus giving every girl in America the illusion that she could someday be "Mrs. Peter Brown." That was good for business, and it showed by the huge number of posters sold, no doubt lining the bedroom walls of teenage girls across America (including my co-author's wife, so I'm told).

But I couldn't be bothered by such trivial matters. I was nuts about Diane and wanted to be with her every moment. That said, I still wasn't totally convinced on the idea of marriage. I must have had some sense in that testosterone-fueled brain of mine. So when Diane pushed for a wedding date, I hatched a plan to maintain my singular status, sort of "having my cake and eating it too."

"Honey," I said, "they want me for this new cowboy show, *Lawman*. In fact, the pilot episode was just sent to New York. Now it usually takes two to three years for a show to make it on the air, so you need to be patient. But the instant this thing sells, we'll get hitched."

There! I figured I was safe. I mean, what were the odds of this new western with a novice-actor in one of the leading roles getting on national television and running every week? Probably slim and none.

Diane, however, beamed when I told her this.

Poor thing, I thought. *She has no clue as to the workings of the real world.*

Apparently, neither did I.

Three days later, R.J. Reynolds bought the entire show. The pilot was sold.

I got drunk that night.

The wedding was set for October 11. There was so much to do; Diane scurried about making all the preparations. She seemed so happy, yet there were times when she'd get real quiet. Eventually we'd "talk."

"Peter," Diane would say, "just who's this wedding for anyhow? For us or for everyone else?"

I had to admit she had a point.

Then out of the blue, Warners scheduled me for an October personal appearance tour to promote *Lawman*. That was going to cause havoc with our wedding plans, but the studio, being the studio, didn't give a rat's ass. It was their subtle way of trying to keep us apart.

So I said, "Screw it! Let's run off to Las Vegas and get married. There's no way they're keeping the two of us apart."

And so we did.

Only when we got there, we couldn't prove we were of age, so no one would marry us. We were a couple of young looking puppies. So there we were, sitting on our suitcases, trying to figure out what to do.

After a bit of scrambling, we got the necessary paperwork, found a justice of the peace, and on Saturday, September 6, 1958, Diane and I became husband and wife. I was twenty-two years young, she was twenty-three. We got married in a strange town with no friends or family present in an empty chapel. But we knew that marriage is for the two people involved and that the love between them is all that counts. When Diane and I whispered our "I do's," it was a moment for the ages.

One month later, on my twenty-third birthday, *Lawman* hit the airwaves and it quickly became a hit. I guess that officially made me an adult: I was a bona fide TV star and I had just married the woman I would love forever.

"Forever" lasted less than two years.

Things were rocky right from the start. The last week in January we moved into our new home thinking that would make everything better. It didn't.

Two weeks later, our situation came to a head. Only married five months, we decided to separate. We soon reconnected and tried to give it a another go. But by then, I could see what a mistake it was to marry at such a young age. Our separate careers had us apart so often, it was really too much to overcome. Had we been ten-years older, more mature, we might have made it. But we were just kids.

I had bought us a beautiful home on Mandalay Drive in Encino Hills, so that's where we had tried to play "house." But we just didn't get along. It wasn't any one thing you could put your finger on. We never threw plates, hardly ever raised our voices. But the excitement was just not there. Even the sex was not good, which was almost impossible to believe once you took a look at Diane.

There was one time, however, after we had been apart for awhile that things became sexually charged. Diane had flown back to town and I had picked her up at the airport. But instead of going right home, for some reason we just drove around, finally ending up on Mulholland Drive. We parked in a secluded spot and then something came over us.

We were like two horny teenagers chomping at the bit. Of course, we weren't that far from being teenagers, and "horny" was definitely in the building. The sex we had that night in the car was out of this world. After the third time, we both struggled to sit up, our bodies soaking wet from the sweat of this most extreme work-out. She sat close to me as I drove home. I soon realized, however, that evening in the car was better than anything we had ever done at home or would ever do again anywhere. We were never able to replicate the intensity of the feelings of that one night.

Finally, pretty much amicably, we divorced in 1959. We told people that it was due to career conflicts, but I think if we had both really loved each other, we could have survived anything. That just wasn't the case.

The divorce cost me a powder blue Cadillac convertible and a house. Over the years, we ran into each other on occasion. There was never any animosity, but we both seemed to want these infrequent meetings to end as quickly as possible. I think each of us was a little embarrassed. And really, we were just too damn young.

For five years, I was off the marriage wagon. This didn't mean I turned into a monk or anything. When you get thrown from a horse, you have to get right back on, or you'll always fear that horse. I got right back on the horse.

There were a lot of women then. In April of 1961, I dated Teri Janssen, a former Miss Los Angeles who had been crowned Miss California that year. She later competed in the Miss Universe competition. Teri was the half-sister of David Janssen; a couple of years later, David would go on to star in the mega-hit TV show, *The Fugitive.* That show's final episode in 1967 was watched by more people than any other television show in history at the time.

But I digress . . . now let's see, where was I? Oh yeah, Teri. My memory of our relationship is a little bit foggy, but it couldn't have been too intense. A month after we dated, she married another guy.

Moving on.

Then there was Suzanne Lloyd whose stepfather was S. Sylvan Simon, the famous producer/director. They lived in Beverly Hills. In the "It's a Small World" category, Suzanne went on to marry orchestra leader Buddy Bregman. Their daughter Tracey is now a soap opera actress on *The Young and the Restless* and was on *The Bold and the Beautiful,* both shows I had been on some twenty years earlier.

Although I really didn't get to know Suzanne that well, the one thing that sticks out in memory was the ring she gave me. It was her stepfather's and bore the letters "SSS" on it. For reasons still beyond my comprehension, she insisted I take it, that it was important to her for me to have it. Who was I to argue with this strikingly beautiful lady? To this day, I still have that ring somewhere.

Other actresses, models, and starlets came and went. I have great memories of Kathie Browne, a tall, blonde actress I dated off and on for quite a while. And there were many others. But none of them meant enough for me to want to get really involved, at least not until three years after my divorce from Diane. It was then that a bombshell hit me. I developed the most intense feelings for a woman that I had ever experienced. The memories of her and our lost love haunt me to this day.

It was 1962 when Kyoko Takahashi stole my heart. I had just finished filming *Merrill's Marauders* in the Philippines when a wild idea flew into my head. Having no immediate obligations to tie me down, I thought I'd have an adventure by going to Hong Kong and Tokyo before heading back to L.A.

During the making of the movie, we had been out in the jungle a lot. Because of unpredictable weather, the remote shooting sites, and dealing with the locals, it had been very difficult to stay on any kind of a rigid schedule. Many times we worked twleve to sixteen hours a day to try to catch up. We ended our shooting schedule six days late, mostly due to the bad weather. But on the plus side, that bad weather meant a lot of overtime pay. It was a substantial amount.

After the wrap, I marched into the studio accountant's office which was actually just a small trailer. Behind a tiny desk wedged between overstuffed file cabinets was a small, thin Asian man poring over spreadsheets. His shirt was soaked with sweat. When I entered, he looked up and knew who I was right away.

"So, I've got some overtime pay coming, don't I?" I asked.

He shuffled a bunch of papers, finally pulling out a sheet that had my info. He held it close to his face and read it up and down, his lips moving silently as he went. He set the paper down, then looked up and smiled.

"You have over $10,000 coming to you."

Well, isn't that nice? I thought.

My plan was coming together. However, being as young and inexperienced as I was, I wasn't sure what was allowable. I almost felt like I was doing something illegal.

"Can I draw it out?"

"Can you draw it out?" he echoed. "Can you draw it out?!" There was a long pause. Then . . . "Of course you can draw it out. Wait right here."

Before I knew it, I was on a plane to Hong Kong with over $10,000 stuffed inside my coat pocket. It was the most money I ever had on me.

The studio had originally purchased a first-class ticket that would take me from the Philippines to Los Angeles. But I was able to trade that ticket for one in coach class that would get me to Hong Kong and Tokyo with enough left over to still qualify me for a first-class ticket for that long trip home across the ocean. I smiled as the plane took off. This was the first opportunity I ever experienced where I really had ample time and money for myself and I was going to take advantage of it.

After landing in Hong Kong, the main thing I did was to go clothes shopping. I wanted to, had to, look good! I had a pair of elegant suits custom made, the cost of which was a fraction of the price back in the states.

From there, it was on to Tokyo. Once at my hotel, I was checking out the lobby when I spotted a newspaper lying on a chair. It was all in Japanese, but a picture of a man on the front page caught my eye. I looked once, twice, then picked up the paper and held it close to my face.

"This can't be him," I muttered. "What are the odds?"

But it was him. The picture was of Robert Fuller, my *Lawman* buddy and the enabler of my horse's alcoholic tendencies, right there on the front page of the Tokyo newspaper.

Oh, this is too good to be true, I thought.

I took the paper over to the hotel clerk and insisted he tell me why my friend Robert Fuller was on the front page of his city's newspaper. The translation was a little sketchy, but from what he said, I gathered that Robert was doing a show, some cowboy western type thing, at the nearby Coliseum. I found out where the Coliseum was and immediately cabbed over there.

My run of dumb luck continued. The security people at the Coliseum gate somehow recognized me. Unlike today's security conscious mania, these people not only let me in the building, they actually unlocked Robert's dressing room door and allowed me to wait in there.

The Coliseum resembled the Capitol Records building in L.A., kind of like a big stack of LP records (for those of you who remember what LP's look like). Robert's dressing room was up a couple of flights, so it had a balcony.

Very nice! I thought.

I noticed his holster and gun hanging on a chair.

Oh, this just keeps getting better and better.

I strapped the holster around my waist, checked his gun, and then went out on the balcony. I looked like a real cowboy doof.

Soon enough, I spied Robert on the street below getting out of a cab. Re-entering the room, I hid behind a pillar. I heard the door open, then close. I waited a moment, then leaped out from behind the pillar.

"DRAW!" I yelled as I pulled his gun out of its holster.

I startled the shit out of him. I'm sure for an instant, he thought he was about to be robbed. The look on his face was priceless.

"You son-of-a-bitch!" he yelled as a smile finally broke out across his face. "What the hell are you doing here?!"

I was halfway around the world in a country totally foreign to the ways of the U.S. and here I was playing "cowboy" with a long-time friend. Does it get any better than that?

We quickly caught up, then Robert announced that he was taking me out to a party at the home of the president of Toei Studios, a Japanese film, television production, and distribution company. I was game for anything. The adventure continued.

It was an outdoor garden party, only this garden was about the size of the Rose Bowl. People of every nationality milled about and there were chefs everywhere, each preparing and serving his own particular specialty. I went up to the first chef and he handed me a plate of some kind of exotic seafood, maybe squid. Who knew?

He stood there and waited for me to eat it. Being the adventurous good sport I am, I gave it a try. Amazingly enough, it was excellent. He smiled before moving on to the next person. This continued with all the other chefs.

Robert and I made small talk with some studio big shots . . . at least I assumed they were big shots. I couldn't always tell as English was spoken only intermittently.

Eventually, me being me, I gravitated to the ladies. And there were a ton of pretty girls there. I wandered and smiled, smiled and wandered, just like a kid in a candy shop. Even if they couldn't understand me, the ladies were unfailingly polite and happy, always pleasant when conversing, their gentle voices making me think I understood what they were saying in a foreign language of which I had not one whit of comprehension.

And then, I met Kyoko.

And somehow, the Earth moved.

Kyoko Takahashi was an actress, a contract player at Toei. And she was a knockout, a tremendously gorgeous, satin doll. And fortunately for me, for us, she spoke some English.

I immediately saw how elegant yet funny she was. We hit it off right away. Since it was obvious that everything in her country was so new and different to me, Kyoko made it her mission to enhance my education concerning all things Japanese. And I was a most willing student. I had never fallen in love so quickly or so completely.

For the next week, we were inseparable. She showed me her town, both the historical buildings and the wondrous countryside. I forget what we actually did because I was so enraptured by her beauty. She was all I could think about.

Unfortunately for my love-life, I had to get back to the states and *Lawman*. On that fateful last day, Kyoko drove me to the airport; it was raining just like in *Casablanca* . . . to be clear, I was "Rick" and she was "Ilsa."

At most airports back then, you'd walk right out on the tarmac to get on your plane. There was not much security or full body searches back in those days.

Up to that point, the week had been nothing but elegance, courtesy, and love. That made my departure so much more difficult. We were both crying as I kissed her good-bye; rain dripped off our noses. I climbed to the top of the portable stairs leading into the airplane, then turned and waved to her. My heart was breaking.

This incredible moment was abruptly shattered by the rudest American stewardess I have ever come across. I was carrying some large souvenirs onto the plane. This clown virtually threw herself in front of me and announced most imperiously that I could not bring those items onto the plane. She was so loud that the other passengers froze. All eyes were on me.

Unfortunately, my *Casablanca* moment was destroyed. After the wonderful week with Kyoko where everything was so pleasant and gracious, and after now having had to leave what could have been the love of my life, it was just too much. This bit of ugly Americana totally pissed me off.

"Screw this and screw you!" I shouted at the startled attendant.

Dropping everything, I wheeled around and marched off the plane. The befuddled stewardess looked on in confusion.

Kyoko was still on the tarmac. Her eyes widened as she watched me stomp down the stairs.

"I'm staying!" I boldly announced.

And for a moment, there was a glimmer of hope as we stared into each others' eyes. But reality reared its ugly head almost right away. We both knew I had to be on that plane. I hugged her hard and long one last time, then turned and re-boarded the airplane without ever looking back. I paid no attention to the obnoxious stewardess.

I knew that my one-week love story was over. Oh, we wrote back and forth for awhile; I wanted her to fly to the U.S. while she thought I could maybe get work at the Toei studio. But we both had obligations in our own countries. It was just not meant to be.

I never saw Kyoko again.

O.K., back to America, my career, and the rest of my wives.

Dick Davis was a friend who was a bit of a "player"; and that's really saying something coming from me. He had a floating bachelor pad that also doubled as a boat. He christened it "With Vigah."

One Sunday afternoon during the mid-sixties, Dick brought a statuesque brunette over to my place for cocktails. She was a knockout. Sandra Edmundson worked as a model, having been a cover girl for several magazines. She was a very classy lady. For the first time in several years, I was enchanted by a young woman. Her relationship with Dick couldn't have been too serious, because when I asked her out, she said "Yes!" right away.

We dated for awhile. I guess that didn't piss off Dick too much since he's still a friend today.

Sandra was a good person whom I really liked a lot. Since I had already done the marriage thing once and managed to survive, I figured, *What the hell, why not try it again?* I asked, she again said, "Yes!", and like that, we were engaged.

On May 26, 1964, Sandra and I got married in a church on a hill in Palos Verdes. In a year, we had our first child. We named him "Matthew Peter Brown." I was absolutely thrilled with being a dad. The husband thing? Not so much. I don't remember any specific problems Sandra and I had. We just grew apart. By 1969, I was again a single man.

After the divorce, I stayed very involved with my son. I may have been done being a husband, at least temporarily, but I was always up for being a dad. Unfortunately, I was not able to maintain sterling relations with Sandra. She actually preferred that I not be so involved with Matt, that I not come to his baseball and basketball games.

That wasn't going to happen.

It would seem to make sense that two civilized people, sharing the greatest of all treasures, a son or a daughter, would be able to maintain a cordial relationship with each other throughout the major events of their offspring's life: graduation, marriage, grandchildren. Regrettably, we didn't. I have not spoken to Sandra in years.

You'd think I'd be shying away from marriage after two divorces by the age of thirty-five. And once again, you'd be wrong.

On November 14, 1971, during the beginning of my run on *Days of Our Lives*, I married model Yvette Safargy at the Beverly Hills Presbyterian Community Church. As was the case during wedding number two, my brother Phil handled the best man duties. I was thirty-six and Yvette was thirty-one. We were both old enough to know what we wanted. This one was going to work for sure.

Yvette Liliane Safargy was born in Shanghai, China, raised in Australia, and modeled in France. She had a slight accent, but for the life of me I could never tell what it was. We ended up being married for just a couple of years.

I met Yvette at The Candy Store. No, I wasn't on the prowl for young girls. The Candy Store was an upscale bar on Cannon Drive in Beverly Hills. There was an actual candy counter in the bar and Yvette, that little sweetie, was the candy counter clerk.

Yvette was just as cute as she could be. I got to know her over a period of time, always saying "Hi!" whenever I saw her. One night the place wasn't too busy, so we talked for quite a while. She seemed like such a great person.

Finally, I had to go. At the time, I was driving my 1951 Bentley. I was at least five miles away from The Candy Store, but I could not get her out of my mind. Like that, I made a life-altering decision. I cranked the steering wheel hard to the left and did an emergency U-turn. Within minutes, I was back at The Candy Store. She was still at her counter but was beginning to close up shop.

"So, Yvette," I blurted out breathlessly while trying to appear nonchalant, "would you like to come back to my house for a couple of drinks?"

The question just hung in the air.

"I suppose," she whispered demurely. A wry smile crossed her face.

We had one drink at my place, then another, then yet still another. Somehow, a month went by and she was still there. This was a new record for the length of any of my one-night stands.

In December of 1970, we were still together. That was when I moved to Malibu and rented an apartment at 22626 Pacific Coast Highway. Yvette, along with my worldly possessions, came along for the ride. She never went home.

Our honeymoon was legendary, at least for me. The day after the wedding, the two of us flew to Venezuela for a movie I was doing. *Piranha! Piranha!* was the name of the movie; I was shooting it with my good buddy from *Laredo*, William Smith. It was actually William who had gotten me the role. Bill Gibson was the writer and our director.

Our first stop was at the Caracas Hilton where we would be staying. It was very nice, but somehow not nice enough for Yvette. We weren't there forty-eight hours before she wanted to go home. She missed her friends and she missed L.A. She whined constantly. We had been married less than a week.

I should have seen it coming.

For one set of scenes, we had to get on a plane and go to Columbia to some diamond mines. I had to take Yvette along; after all, it was our honeymoon. The base camp for the shoot was actually an import/export terminal for exotic animals. Once there, Yvette fell in love with a monkey . . . that would be "another" monkey. She named him "*Papillon*." That monkey saved our marriage, at least for several weeks. The little guy totally distracted Yvette. The whining, at least about our honeymoon, stopped.

We had a good cast and crew including one of the top special effects guys in the business, Rick Baker. He's gone on to win more awards for makeup than anyone else in the industry, taking the first Oscar ever for makeup in 1982 for his efforts in the horror film *An American Werewolf in London*. For us, he created an incredible visual of a head being eaten by a piranha.

The actual making of the movie was smooth enough, although it became a major problem in our altogether too-short married life. I know that honeymoons are supposed to be a beginning; in our case, it was a beginning, only it was a beginning of the end.

Yvette tried, she really did. She even took acting lessons in the hope that we could work together doing movies for my company, Redwine International. But she never really became an actress; she didn't want to pay the price. So I did.

Divorce number three.

Yvette now lives in Palm Springs. We haven't spoken in ages. So it goes. But on the plus side (?), I got *Papillon* in the divorce. Oh, those custody battles are really tricky, especially when there's a monkey involved. I have no idea now why I even wanted him. It must have been that I was so good with animals, I guess.

I kept Papillon in an eight feet by eight feet by ten feet cage. It really was no way for him to live, but I just didn't have the time to devote to him. I knew a guy, Ralph Helfer, who owned a company out in the hills that supplied animals for the movies, so I gave Papillon to Ralph instead of Yvette. We do not stay in touch . . . I'm talking about Yvette. The monkey sends me a card every Fathers' Day.

BA DUMP-BUMP!

I had learned my lesson about marriage, so when the next beautiful woman happened by on that treadmill called "my life," I cleverly did not, and I repeat DID-NOT marry her. Oh sure, we may have lived together, maybe even produced a son between the two of us, but we did not get married. I was getting smarter, don't you think?

Jean Carlson McKay and I had a relationship from 1974 to 1979, although for those five years, I knew her as "Amber." She later adopted the name of "Amber Ray" when she was getting a little goofy. I don't know, maybe it was me that was getting a little goofy. Maybe we're all a little goofy. Who knows?

Let's keep going.

Amber and I met when I had an apartment at the Shoreham Towers on Sunset near Tower Records. I was minding my own business one morning just lolling about with a cup of coffee and the morning paper. I headed out to the balcony to enjoy some morning air. I was up a few stories with a great view of the city while overlooking the apartment complex's swimming pool. I was enjoying the day when I happened to look down and noticed a figure swimming in the pool. At that moment, I was no longer minding my own business.

I went down to the pool deck to get a closer look. In the water swimming laps was a long legged, beautiful girl. I sat down nearby and introduced myself. That's how these things get started.

Her name was "Amber" and she was a wannabe actress and model. We talked. Everything I said seemed to make her laugh.

A good audience I thought.

Before I knew it, my "good audience" had moved in.

Boy these things go fast.

Soon we (read: "I") bought a house. That place brings back some very fond memories for me. When I had initially checked it out, I noticed an extremely nice pool table down in the lower level. Being the astute judge of real estate that I was, I told the owner I'd buy the house, but only if the pool table came with it. Ever the hard bargainer, I came away with my pool table and a bit-too-expensive house. But I was happy as was Amber.

The house was on the valley side of Mulholland Drive. One of

With son Joshua

the most distinct memories I have of our new home occurred on a night when I was there alone. I had just consumed a rum and coke at the house bar and paired that with a hit of pot before going for an evening swim in the pool. My mind must have been on heightened alert, because when I went back in the house into the large room on the lower level, I saw a vision. Oh, it wasn't anything as great as seeing an image of Jesus or even Raquel Welch. What I saw that night was a vision of bookcases, giant floor-to-ceiling bookcases, the kind that you need a ladder with wheels attached in order to quickly access all your books on all levels. The bookcases would encircle the room. The next day at the studio, I asked a friend, one of the equipment guys, if he would build them for me. We haggled back and forth a bit, then finally agreed on him building my mystical book holders in exchange for a case of Jack Daniel's Tennessee Whiskey. The bookcases turned out beautifully, exactly the way I envisioned them. That was over thirty-five years ago. It's funny the things you remember.

In January of 1977, we had a son. Joshua Jacob Brown was a wonderful baby. I figured my life was now complete. I just knew I had a great life ahead with Amber.

Within two years, she and Josh were gone.

After the baby was born, Amber changed. She went from being someone I loved, my very best friend, to a complete stranger. It's hard to put your finger on exactly what it was, but our relationship no longer worked. She took Josh and moved to Oyster Bay, New York, on Long Island. That made it very difficult for me to see my second son.

I'd like to think I always maintained a good relationship with Amber, but the move across country really hurt. I'm not sure if it was because we never got married. At the time, she wasn't particularly forthcoming with details. She's no longer with us now, so I guess I'll never get my answers.

I was once again a soldier in the army of single men. I proceeded to make it for twelve years between the dates of my last divorce and my next wedding. That would be my fourth marriage if you're keeping score.

In March of 1984, I was playing in the Michael Landon Celebrity Tennis Tournament. Michael's tournament was staged to benefit four charities in the city of Tucson.

At the tournament, I became totally enamored with one Mary Kathleen Gauba. She was cute as a button, pleasant and perky, and an excellent tennis player. There was, however, a significant chronological difference in our ages; she was born about the same year as my son Matthew. Her sister and two brothers were great people; they seemed to like me and had no problems with my age. And so what if I was forty-eight and she was twenty? I was in great physical condition, had aged well (my opinion), and was very compatible with her. We were both big into athletics, especially tennis, as well as a shared love of horses and the outdoors. With all that in common versus the age disparity, the question was, "Should we get married?" The answer for me was obvious:

Certainly!

I made Mary wife number four on November 29, 1986, Thanksgiving weekend, in Santa Fe, New Mexico. We were married in, of all places, an art gallery. Never let it be said I did anything the conventional way.

The Fenn Gallery was owned by Forrest Fenn, a man I met while on a celebrity junket to Santa Fe. One day during the junket, the "celebs" were given a choice of either touring a state park or going to an art gallery. For whatever reason, I chose the art gallery which Forrest owned.

Forrest Fenn was a wonderful man. As so often happens with me, we became great friends quickly. He had a spectacular garden at his gallery, so when it came time for Mary and me to get married, Forrest suggested we use his garden. I had already tried a Las Vegas wedding chapel and two churches, so I figured, *What have I got to lose?*

He arranged for us to have a huge honeymoon suite with a great steam shower. On the day of the wedding, the weather turned quite cold, not uncommon for Santa Fe in November, so we moved the ceremony into the gallery library. It was a wonderful day.

I guess I had learned a few things during my first half-century on the planet, because this marriage endured. It was easily the most successful one to date. We were married for thirteen years (Remember, that's "91" in dog-years). We lived in an oh-so scenic four-story townhouse overlooking the Pacific; I had a home gym which I used to stay in peak physical condition while Mary enjoyed our multiple deck patios where she could raise her plants. And we had the pitter-patter of little feet clattering on the hardwood floors to make our family complete . . . oh, it's not what you're thinking. We shared our home with the stray animals we had picked up through the years: a dog and six cats. The dog was a real mutt; I named him "Canarly" because as I so often said, "You canarly (can hardly) tell what breed he is."

Mary and I were happy for so many years, both of us very giving to the other. The greatest gift Mary ever gave me was a constant, ever-present smile. I just loved looking at it. Mary said the best gift I ever gave her was "freedom." This always confused me a bit. I think she believed that once you got married, you couldn't go here or there, or you couldn't do this or that, at least not without spousal permission. But that, of course, just wasn't how I thought. For me, the old adage, "If you love something, set it free, yadda, yadda, yadda" applied to both partners.

It helped that we both liked the same stuff, played so well together, and it didn't hurt that we lived near the beach.

Or so I thought.

"I hate L.A.," she would say more than once.

"You're not in L.A.," I would respond just as often. "You're in Hermosa Beach. We're just a half-mile from the ocean."

I just couldn't convince her she wasn't in L.A. even though we tried to counteract the hurry-up L.A. lifestyle by biking and hiking and playing tennis and golf. It just didn't work.

At one point, we established a long-range plan for us to move to Colorado, Montana, or New Mexico. I even bought forty acres outside of Ridgway, Colorado, saying that I'd rather reside there and keep an apartment in L.A. than the other way around. I did like the idea of living there with just my wife, my animals, and my friends . . . long-range, of course. Probably too long-range for Mary.

For whatever reasons, she always hated living in L.A. She was definitely more of a small town girl and had always wanted to go back to live in Aspen, Colorado, where she was from. That was the ultimate dream. It was also the ultimate cause of our downfall, although other reasons surely existed.

This most successful marriage of mine to date ended in 1999. I gave her our Volkswagen bus; I loved that van. Everything else was split fifty-fifty. She went on to marry a nice guy named Pete and they have one daughter. It seems that she now has everything she ever wanted as they settled in Kilauea, Hawaii . . .

Wait, . . . what? Let me look at that again:

"They settled in Kilauea, Hawaii."

Really?! What the hell is she doing in Hawaii?!

For as many times as she told me we had to move to Colorado, she then ended up in Hawaii.

Go figure.

Let's skip ahead to now. I've saved the best for last, not just because I consider it to be the best but more that I plan on it being the last . . . the last marriage of Peter Brown (Sounds like an independent movie title, doesn't it?).

I met the German born Kerstin Kern at the cowboy fan-centric "National Festival of the West" at WestWorld, a horse event site in Scottsdale, Arizona. KK (as I affectionately call her; she became "KK" after I had trouble pronouncing her name. I kept calling her, "KAIR-stin," and she kept correcting me. Since I always signed my e-mails "P.B.", she began signing hers "KK" Thus, a nickname was born).

The "National Festival of the West" is going on twenty-two years now. It's all things western for all western fans: a music jamboree, cowboy competitions, a trade show, cowboy poetry, a chuck wagon cook-off, film festival, et al. They add more events every year. They're also very big on having the western TV and film stars of the fifties and sixties there to sign autographs and talk to the fans. And although I hate to admit it, I am one of those "stars of yesteryear."

It was March 15, 2001. My autograph booth was next to Bruce Boxleitner's. Bruce had been one of the leads in the television series *How the West Was Won* which was largely why he was there. For this discussion of KK, however, it's more important to note

With KK at 2002 Western Legends Round-up, Kanab, Utah.

that he'd been a co-star along with Kate Jackson on the TV series *Scarecrow and Mrs. King*, an offbeat spy drama.

KK was there to see Bruce, not me. She had no idea who I was, hard as that is to believe (The fact that *Lawman* had been off the air for eight years before she was born may have had something to do with it), nor did she know any of the other cowboy celebrities at the autograph tables. KK had been a fan of Bruce's since she was fourteen-years-old growing up in Germany; she loved watching him in *Scarecrow and Mrs. King* dubbed in German. Bruce's appearance at WestWorld that year was the first time she had ever seen him in person.

KK had a great spot in front of Bruce's table and was not about to give it up. I noticed her right away. I tend to notice all gorgeous redheads right away. (She now claims I didn't notice her. I guess we'll just have to agree to disagree on that point.) During a slow moment when Bruce had stepped away, she said "Hi!" to me and asked if I would sign a photo she had of our group of cowboys doing mounted shooting, so I signed it for her. We exchanged some small talk but then Bruce returned, the show went on, and we went our separate ways. (Amazingly enough, years later when we did get married, Bruce came to our wedding, but I'm getting ahead of myself here.)

In March of '02, KK returned to see Bruce again. Unbeknownst to her and most of the staff at the National Festival of the West, Bruce had canceled his appearance on short notice after being hired for an acting job. Those always took precedent over fan shows. KK, not aware of Bruce's cancellation, continued to stand in front of his autograph table. At one point, she asked a volunteer where Bruce was; he said he'd check it out.

While KK was waiting, I arrived to begin setting up my table. I spotted her immediately. I definitely liked the look of this pretty redhead.

"Hey, I remember you," I said.

KK made a show of looking at my name tag, then remembered me autographing her picture the previous year. She still had no idea who I was.

(Again, really?!).

At least she had figured out that if I was up there on the stage, I must be someone memorable, so she introduced herself. We touched for the first time as we shook hands. (Several years later, I finally confessed that while I didn't really remember her, I did like her aura, so I figured I'd give it a shot).

"Do you have wheels?" I asked, a strange question for me to be posing to this pretty lady.

"Well, uh, yes I do," she answered.

"Is there a stationery store nearby?"

"Yes, there's a Staples just down the road."

I kept the conversation flowing.

"It seems I've run out of gold and silver autographing pens.

Would you be so kind as to get me some more?"

"Sure!" she replied.

I gave her a twenty and off she went. This was really nothing new to her. KK had been at four of Bruce's previous events, two in California and two in Arizona; she had become familiar enough with the operation that she had even helped him out from time to time. The married KK was separated when we met, so she could do as she pleased. And she was pleased to get me my pens.

Originally, KK thought nobody knew about these western shows, but she soon saw that there was a real audience for them, and that the competition for autographs was big. Devoted fans needed to commit a considerable amount of time to secure their desired signatures. On this particular day, KK had taken the day off from work. She had already paid her $10 entrance fee, so there would be no problem re-entering. When I asked my favor of her, she figured, *Why not?*

When KK returned with the pens, I had a picture taken of her and me, this time with my arm around her. She enjoyed the attention. While knowing I was indeed famous, she still didn't have any frame of reference regarding what I had done to accomplish such notoriety (I've got to quit harping on that).

As a thank-you for getting the pens, I gave her an autographed picture of myself, personalized with her name on it. Unfortunately, I misspelled "Kerstin." Horrified at this gaffe, I immediately offered to sign another one for her.

"Oh, that's O.K.," she said. "You can just write "Oops!" on this one." To this day, she still has the "Oops" picture.

I appreciated not only her graciousness in making me feel comfortable but also her humor. At the bottom, I did write "Oops", then re-autographed it spelling her name correctly this time.

"Thank you so much," she said.

"Are you going to hang around?" I asked hopefully.

"Yes," she replied. Then a thought struck her. "I'll be right back."

With that, she took off and drove home. A half hour later, she returned, this time bearing all of the photos she had taken at the previous year's festival. She wanted me to see them. I was quite touched by her efforts. I needed to see more of this woman.

"So, uh, do you want to walk with me down to the horse pen?"

Smooth, huh?

Amazingly enough, she agreed to go with me and my buddy, actor Alex Cord, down to see a local horse trainer. We were both very interested in the work he was doing with the horses.

While the three of us were there, I bought KK a glass of wine. When I handed her the wine glass, I noticed she was wearing quite a few rings on quite a variety of fingers. The inevitable question was itching to be asked.

"Are you married?"

Now for a bit of payback.

"No," she answered, although truth be told, while she was separated, technically she was still married. The divorce had not yet been finalized, although KK wasn't really all that worried about it. She was more concerned with finding out about this very kind and charming gentleman . . . to clarify, that would be me.

With our first "walk-to-the-horse-pen" date over, KK went off to check out the rest of the festival while I went back to work. I had trouble getting her out of my mind. Several times during the day she'd come by the booth just to say "Hi." On her third trip by, "How about having dinner with a bunch of us?" I asked. "We'd be going with singer Rusty Richards and his wife and also Robert Fuller and Alex Cord."

KK agreed and several hours later she found herself at a table full of western stars at a restaurant called "The Coyote Grill." We had a wonderful and fun dinner. KK ended up spending most of the weekend with me, but with the understanding that there were no strings attached. We both made that apparent from the beginning. I found out later that saying good-bye was far more difficult for KK than for me, even though she had tried not to get too attached. After all, how can you resist a charmer like me? I'm kind of like a lost puppy dog that way.

We stayed in touch through e-mail as a long-distance, non-committed relationship began. KK began driving to L.A. to visit me at my ranch. Soon the visits grew longer and longer, made possible by the convenience of modern technology. KK was now able to work remotely from anywhere, the "anywhere" just referenced being my ranch.

In 2005, KK helped me move out of L.A. I had a business venture supposedly waiting for me in Oklahoma. We drove in tandem to her place in Peoria, Arizona, where I stayed for a couple of days before continuing on to my new home in Oklahoma. At least, that was the plan.

In October, KK was planning a big seventieth birthday bash for me. Since nothing had happened with my supposedly lucrative Oklahoma deal, she suggested I spend the week with her. I thought about it for a nanosecond.

Why not stay with this wonderful lady while waiting for the business venture to come through? I thought.

So, I did . . . and somehow, I never left.

It was just like the play, *The Man Who Came to Dinner*. Needless to say, the opportunity in Oklahoma fell through, but I didn't care. I realized how much I loved being in Arizona . . . and how much I loved being with this redhead.

When I told my kids I was getting married, one of them offered us the use of their beautiful backyard in lovely Newbury Park, California. So on September 6, 2008, exactly fifty years to the day after my first marriage, Kerstin Kern and I were joined in Holy wedlock. As she walked down the makeshift aisle, I was excited and moved at what I thought:

Here and today, KK is going to be my last redhead.

"Do what you love."
— My career advice to
all my children

Chapter 7
My Kids

"Previously on *The Fastest Gun in Hollywood: The Peter Brown Story* . . . " In 1964, Sandra and I got married in a church on a hill in Palos Verdes. In a year, we had our first child . . . I was absolutely thrilled with being a dad.

That paragraph from way back in the last chapter was just to remind you of what I said and to use it as a springboard to delve into a favorite part of one guy's life: my kids. So let's get on with it.

Sandra and I were married at the Crystal Cathedral just south of Los Angeles. On November 10, 1965, a month after I turned thirty, the true proof of my becoming an adult made his way into my life: Matthew Peter Brown, my first son. It was the most exciting thing that had ever happened to me.

Sandra and I divorced in 1969 when Matt was just three-years-old. There was no crying or overt sadness by my little boy. He never seemed down, even when his mom was dating or had gotten remarried, even when he really didn't like the person she had again agreed to share eternal bliss (Too snarky?). Although Matt didn't mourn the loss of his family, I did find out years later that he sometimes fantasized about Sandra and me staying married. He wished for some sort of alternate-universe marriage where we would have been happy. I like to think Matt was too smart to be upset by the divorce, but it was probably more that he was too young to realize the ramifications of what was happening. Either way, I stayed very involved with him. I was always being a dad no matter where I was.

Sandra and I were now tied together for life whether we liked it or not. She fell more into the "not" category than I did. I guess you'd call our relationship "frosty but cordial." Her anger toward me increased enough in later years that she didn't want me to come to Matt's high school baseball or basketball games at the Brentwood Academy in the town of Brentwood, although I'm guessing this had more to do with Larry, her control-freak husband, who wanted her and Matt to have nothing to do with me. The two of them tried to obstruct Matt and my relationship, but guess what?

It didn't work!

That's enough about wife number two. This chapter is supposed to be about my kids, a much more favorable subject of mine.

I loved doing stuff with Matt. I had a big fish tank that took a lot of time and effort to maintain. But even as a little boy, Matt helped to take care of it. It was always important to him that we do it together. We had a nice swing set in the backyard. I actually used it for educational purposes, teaching Matt his numbers in Spanish by having him count the times I would swing him. He thought that was so cool.

We had a dog named *Shaggy* that Matt loved. They could spend hours together in the backyard throwing and fetching a ball; in general, Shaggy did the fetching, although not always. Matt developed a close friendship with a neighbor, Logan Byrnes, son of Edd "Kookie" Byrnes who starred on television's *77 Sunset Strip*. These best friends would regularly swim in Edd's pool. Logan and Matt remained tight until about the fourth grade, although it was probably more due to the fact that Edd and I kind of drifted apart as friends.

With infant son Matthew.

A love of baseball was something Matt and I shared along with my dad, Albert. Pop took Matt to Dodgers' opening day games eight years in a row. He taught Matt how to keep score which I think really helps kids learn the game while keeping them from getting bored. All three of us would go to the games. Matt became a fanatic about all things baseball, from collecting the players' bubble gum cards to listening to the games at night on his transistor radio.

A big event was when I would take him to Hollywood Stars Night at either Dodger Stadium or the Big A in Anaheim where the Angels played. These would often be charity games where various celebrities, including yours truly, would play. It was awesome for the kids. They'd get to go down into the dugout and meet the players and coaches. Once Matt was introduced to L.A. Laker great Kareem Abdul Jabbar. That was totally insane seeing my boy, about four feet tall, standing next to the seven-foot Kareem.

I was especially glad that Matt was able to see me play the night I doubled off the wall. This was a major league ballpark, and there I was standing on second with the crowd going crazy. I remember trying to look cool as I stood there, but inside I was all jumping up and down, just like a little kid.

On another night, the Angels were playing the Boston Red Sox. I managed to meet Hall of Famer Jim Rice who was playing for the Sox. I told him about what a huge, crazy baseball fan Matt was. Jim couldn't have been nicer. He even gave me one of his bats to give to Matt. Back up in the stands, I gave the prized souvenir to Matt. He must have been only about five-years-old. Not knowing any better, he began swinging the bat around, nearly clobbering several nearby spectators. We had to take the bat away from him which was not a popular move with Matt. He began yelling and screaming; I think I nearly traumatized the poor kid. He finally calmed down once we promised to give him the bat back after the game. You know, he still has that bat along with one Dodger catch-

With son Matthew.

er Steve Yeager gave him.

Matt also loved Hot Wheels and vanilla ice cream . . . not mixed together, mind you. Once Matt spied a brand new half-gallon container of vanilla ice cream in the freezer.

"Dad, can I have some vanilla?" he asked. It was one of the few times I had to say "No" to my son.

"Sorry, pal. You can have some other flavor. We have to save the vanilla. We need it to 'feed the beast.'"

Poor Matt had no idea what I was talking about. The "beast" was my good friend Ron Ely, the star of *Tarzan* on TV. Ron was part of my regular poker night group. He had such a thing for vanilla ice cream. While the rest of us would be noshing on chips and pretzels, Ron would be sitting at the poker table checking his cards while eating vanilla ice cream directly from the carton.

"When Ron comes over," I said, "all he gets is a half-gallon of vanilla and a spoon. That's "feeding the beast."

The rules of our custody agreement said that I had Matt every other weekend and a month in the summer. This hardly felt like enough time, but I tried to make the most of it anytime we were together. Third wife Yvette was super strict with Matt and I could tell he didn't like it.

"Hey, knock it off!" I'd exclaim on more than one occasion. "Leave him alone!" I wasn't about to let the time we did have together be uncomfortable for Matt.

When he was in about eighth grade, Matt, Amber (with whom I was living with at the time), and I drove my van to Cabo San Lucas, Mexico. It was an awesome one month vacation where we enjoyed the beauty of the countryside, hit the beach every day, paraglided, snorkeled, and swam. The most memorable part, however, was our ferry boat ride across the Sea of Cortez to Puerto Vallarta. It was horrible. There was a cyclone whipping up the waters that day. For some reason, we got placed on a second tier ferry boat that didn't leave port for a day. It was super hot; everyone aboard got grumpy

The Hollywood Stars: Me with Jack Lemmon and Debbie and Pat Boone.

really fast. No sooner had we finally left port than the boat's electric system went down. There was no air conditioning or refrigeration and whatever food they did have soon went bad. The only ice on the boat seemed to be in our cooler. The shipboard customers were reduced to subsisting on peanut butter and crackers.

After a fitful night of little sleep, we awoke when the sun came up and miraculously, we could see land. That right there nearly made it the greatest day ever. Unfortunately on the trip home, we got stopped and shook down by the Mexican police. It wasn't money they wanted, however. They allowed us to pass after seizing all the eight-track tapes I had in the van. I guess that's what we needed to pay for safe passage back home. I was pissed. Young Matt thought it was a great adventure.

Although not often, I sometimes took Matt to work with me. He enjoyed the NBC studios and going on the set of *Days of Our Lives*. He thought it was all so much fun; he had no sense that I was actually working.

Another time I took him with me when I did a series of Pontiac commercials with good friend Joanna Cassidy. Because we were doing shoots in the Mammoth area and in Nevada, I rented an RV for us. Matt had a blast. Sometimes during the shoots, he would even be in the back of the Pontiac which they were filming. Kids just love that kind of stuff.

We had tremendous fun during Matt's high school years. I suppose I was reliving my youth through him, wishing that was how I had grown up. I lived on Manhattan Beach, and I mean right on the beach. It was every young guy's dream location. Weekends were great. Matt and his buddies and their girls would take over the house and then swarm the beach, playing beach volleyball, going body surfing and boogie boarding, just generally having the best fun you could have at the best beach around. It was a great time in my life.

Matt was a tremendous kid, but he grew up (6'3") and became an even better adult. He went to college at Georgetown where he played all the intramurals and, being a California beach kid, even started the volleyball club. He ended up graduating with a degree in American Government before going on to and graduating from Villanova University School of Law. As if you can't tell, I am one proud father.

While I like to think that nothing about the law really intrigued Matt, he corrects me by saying that's not true. It's "justice" that intrigues him and it drives his life. He finds the principles of justice and freedom or liberty very interesting; it's the practice of the law, the litigating or corporate law that he simply found uninteresting. Matt decided there were other ways to pursue his interest in justice.

He's grown up to be an incredibly fair and ethical man.

Matt met his wonderful wife Sarah in New Orleans at, of all places, Mardi Gras. The year was 1990. Matt was in his second year of law school; Sarah was a college junior. Far from being a southern belle, however, she actually was visiting from her home in Berkeley, California. Matt had been invited by a buddy to come down for Mardi Gras. The friend had a lot of room, so he told Matt to invite anybody he wanted. Now, follow this: Matt invited Phillip Williams, one of his Manhattan Beach weekend pals from high school. In turn, Phillip, who was in architecture school at Berkeley, also invited a few friends, one of whom was Sarah. Now it starts getting good.

It was the day after Fat Tuesday. At Phillip's behest, Matt had gone to the airport to pick up Sarah who would be arriving late. As soon as they met, they were so comfortable with each other. They immediately began joking around and soon headed to a bar where dancing ensued. While it was definitely not love at first sight, it was, as Matt so often describes it, "excitement" at first sight. Together, they laughed their heads off that night.

"I knew Matt and I would be friends forever," Sarah told me in later years.

Sarah is one super lady. She has a degree in environmental design, which to me means she's essentially an architect. She's a builder by trade, working as a general contractor. I'm not kidding when I say she can make or build anything. She is quite amazing.

When the school year ended, Matt drove across the country and went directly to Berkeley. By then, they had decided they were totally in love. They've been together ever since.

When Matt graduated from law school, he had to pick a place to take the bar exam. By then, Sarah had graduated from Berkeley. Matt and Sarah had talked about moving in together, but they wanted to go somewhere where neither of them had established any roots. Their relationship was fresh and new, so they wanted to start their life together somewhere that was fresh and new.

Sarah had once been to New Mexico on an archaeological dig and had liked her short time there, so she suggested Santa Fe. Ever agreeable my son, Matt said, "Great!" In rapid succession, he signed up for the bar, went to New Mexico, passed the bar (He also passed the bar in California), moved to New Mexico, and bought a house.

Oh, and they got married, too . . . or should that be "two"? You see, my wacky kids actually got married two times in 1993.

Their first wedding, the legal one, was held on January 23 in the exciting and highly-charged atmosphere of Las Vegas, Nevada. The Graceland Elvis Chapel was the site of their nuptials. Dressed in my cowboy finest, I had the incredible honor of giving the bride away. Sarah's parents weren't in attendance. There was no problem there; they were all for the kids getting married. In fact, they were neither for nor against the Vegas wedding; they just opted to attend the larger, more spiritual wedding in Santa Fe on August 28 of the same year.

Matt had never demonstrated any inclination toward following me in a career in show business. He definitely had no interest in acting, especially after seeing how the industry works. While I loved what constituted my life's passion and was willing to play by their rules (more or less) and roll with the punches, Matt felt that at times I had been blackballed from working, either for sometimes being too old, and other times for not being old enough. For movies and TV, you often have to have the right look at the right time for the right role. I agree with Matt that it can be unsettling to work in a field that has jobs that are many times less based on merit than on external factors over which I had no control (looks).

Matt wanted a career where his actual abilities had more of an influence. He did like the idea of writing or directing. He loves film and is a great storyteller. I'm sure it's part of our shared DNA. However, he never actively pursued a career in the business. At times, he's worked with a buddy on some concepts for TV or film, but those efforts were really more of a hobby for him. My career, judging from what Matt had seen happen to me at times, was not all that attractive to him.

In Santa Fe, Matt got a life-altering job when he had the incredibly good fortune of being chosen for the prestigious position of clerk in the 10th Circuit Court of Appeals for the Honorable Judge Oliver Seth. It was just the greatest job ever for him. He grew to respect the judge immensely and they became life-long friends. Matt had been on the job for about two years when Sarah's family began dealing with some serious health issues, so Matt and Sarah packed up and moved back to Berkeley to be with her family. They've been there pretty much ever since.

Out of the clear blue one day, I got a call from Matt. He sounded a little down, voicing concerns about his career path. He was definitely at a crossroads.

"Dad," he finally asked, "what do I do?"

I quickly donned my Robert Young *Father Knows Best* sport coat, the one with the patches on the elbows (O.K., I'm kidding about that part). I thought back to all the good advice that Pop had given me over the years and this is what I came up with:

"Do what you love."

It was something I was sure I said to my kids all the time, even when they were in high school, but this was the first instance where I was relatively certain one of them was actually listening to me. Matt took that bit of advice and ran with it . . . and he's still running with it.

Matt and wife Sarah were both avid toy collectors when they met. She had amassed a wonderful array of all things Mickey Mouse; Matt liked finding old time comic books. The two of them were always going off to toy stores, antique shops, flea markets, ever on the lookout for fun things to add to their collections. "Fun" was the operative word in their relationship. They were incredible party givers and were always having "game nights" at their house.

So, based on the "Do what you love" wisdom imparted by old Dad, Matt start investigating how to combine what he and Sarah loved with the everyday task of making a living. And soon, he came up with the perfect solution:

He started a toy company.

It was the exact antithesis of what he had prepared for in the legal profession. The reason that Matt didn't like being a lawyer, besides the feeling that it was so tedious and boring, was the adversarial nature of the occupation. The law was a war, often times destructive. Matt had it in him to create something, to make something that mattered. He spiritually hungered to create. While he felt he had no real artistic skills for actual hands-on development, he knew he could create a business . . . a toy business. He did what he loved and it resulted in fifteen years of success and joy in the world of play.

Matt has become a seasoned entrepreneur, although he likes to refer to himself as "a recovering attorney." In 1996 working with the man who invented the brightly colored, snap-together plastic toy called the "Zoob" (stands for Zoology, Ontology, Ontogeny, Botany), they started the Primordial Toy Company with Matt as president. It became very successful selling only to upscale specialty retailers.

On September 6, 1997, Matt and Sarah's daughter, my granddaughter, "Isabella" was born, ensuring that I would finally have someone to bounce on my knee for years to come. That date is such an important one to me. Exactly eleven years later, to the day, KK and I were married.

It was at about this time that Matt left Primordial. It was the sad but all too common story of many partnerships. Matt had a falling out with his partner, so he opted to take a break. It didn't last long.

Matt soon decided he was going to start another company unless Mike Wood, a business friend and CEO/founder of LeapFrog

With son Matt and his family: wife Sarah, mother-in-law Judy, daughter Isabella.

(another toy company), wanted to hire him. Mike's company was the only one Matt would consider working for. From 1999-2001, Matt was vice-president of their internet division which he helped to create. He was also named VP of business development.

In 2002, Matt took some time off. Along with Sarah and growing-up-too-fast Isabella and also their dogs, the young family drove around and camped all over the west. It was during this trip that they bought the land in Santa Fe that would be instrumental in their lives down the line.

At that time, Matt had thought about starting up a candy company; candy and toys . . . it all goes together. But instead, he and some buddies founded "Big Boing," another toy company, in 2003. Matt assumed the title of "Play Czar," which aptly describes his personality. Again, he helmed a very successful company. In 2010, they wrapped up all the day-to-day operations of Big Boing. It now exists solely as a holding company for different assets created by Big Boing.

In late summer of that year, Matt and Sarah were making plans to move to Santa Fe when he received a phone call from the play giant, Scholastic Inc., a global children's publishing, education, and media company. They wanted Matt to be a senior VP of their company as well as president of one of their divisions, Klutz, the publisher of "books plus" for children and other creative activities where he would lead the creative direction of their publishing program and manage strategic development of the Klutz brand. So, on September 7, 2010, Matt accepted both positions.

Although now residing in Berkeley, Matt and Sarah are currently building a house on the twenty-eight acres they own just outside of Santa Fe. It's sort of their dream home, not a place they'll be permanently moving to anytime soon, but more of a family destination, a retreat so to speak, where all family members, KK and I included, can go to relax and enjoy each other and the great outdoors of New Mexico. At some point, it will be a retirement place for Matt and Sarah. At present, my other son Josh, Matt's brother, and Josh's wife Katchie are in the process of moving in to Matt and Sarah's Santa Fe house.

Today Matt serves on the board of GoAnimate, a social-networking animation startup. He has become noted as an expert in play and is named on numerous patents for educational toys, technology, video games, and even candy. But more than anything, Matt is a very proud father and happy husband who also enjoys a renewed relationship with his brother Josh.

Ah, yes, Josh, my other son. He's a wonderful young man . . . a big wonderful young man. Unfortunately, I didn't get to see Josh that much when he was growing up. There's a huge gap in our relationship, one that is still very painful to me, even to this day.

The "spaceship" house.

As you will recall from the previous chapter, I lived with Amber Karlson from 1974-1979 in a house just off Mulholland. I remember the house because it was just down the hill from the spaceship house that was used in the movie *Body Double*. For whatever reason, Matt was infatuated with the spaceship house.

"Pop!" he'd yell at me. I loved that he called me Pop just like Phil and I had called Albert, our father, Pop. "I just shot the spaceship house!" he'd announce. "I hit it three times!"

Like father, like son. Fortunately, the BB gun I had given him could do little damage to the vacant futuristic homestead.

On January 23, 1977, in Los Angeles, Amber and I welcomed my second son into the family. You could tell right away that little Josh Brown was going to be a sizable boy. Sadly, I missed most of seeing him grow to the big man he is today.

Amber and I always had a good relationship, or so I thought. At the least, I felt we were very close friends. But after the baby came, she changed. Maybe it was because we never got married, a little hairier proposition in those days. Whatever it was, things were never the same between us. She even changed her name to "Amber Ray"; don't ask me why. When the eventual split came, she took little Josh and moved a country away, all the way to Oyster Bay, New York.

Working on the west coast as much as I was, it was difficult to say the least to see my second son. When I would visit him, there was more tension between us than there should have been. I attribute this to the fact that this young boy hardly knew who I was. I remember once I took Josh to FAO Schwarz for some toy shopping. It must have been before Christmas. It was so cold out and amazingly there were no cabs to be found. Standing there with my little boy freezing, I got fed up, so I ordered a limousine to take the two of us shopping. It was one of those really big mothers, the kind that seated eight or nine. That was quite the shopping experience.

The other thing about Josh's youth that really hurt was that my two boys did not have the usual love-hate, Ma-he's-looking-at-me sibling relationship that the rest of us so routinely had. Coming from different mothers, being eleven years apart in age, and residing on opposite sides of the country, Matt and Josh had little contact save for the year or so at the beginning of Josh's life. But then a wonderful thing happened when Josh was about seventeen: he wrote his big-brother Matt a letter.

That was a life-altering week for Matt and, really, the entire family. He was in Santa Fe at the time and had just been informed by his mother that she was getting divorced again. On top of that, there was some other family business that was really shaking up the dynamics of the Brown family (more on that later). So when Matt opened up Josh's letter, he thought most of the fireworks were over. . . . only, there was more.

Josh was just coming of age, maturing to the point where he could think more for himself. And his thoughts were with his

Fathers' Day 2012, with sons Josh and Matt.

family. He wanted to know us. He wanted to reconnect with the brother he hardly knew.

That letter was a touchstone in my family's history. Josh stayed in touch with his brother ever since. When Matt and Sarah moved to Berkeley, Josh moved in with them for a year or two. They helped him transition into his new life out there.

It wasn't all one-sided either. Matt thought it was so cool to have a brother again. And while living together, Josh helped in the remodel of Matt and Sarah's house. You might think it could be difficult having a third person in your house for all that time. But Josh, just the opposite of loquacious, was a model roommate.

He's very low key, a private person by nature, who likes movies, hiking, bike rides, dinners, and, in general, just hanging out. He's very meditative and loves nature, being really into the earth. He's become a wonderful gentleman.

Josh has most recently been running the sports division of R.E.I. in Berkeley. He recently married a wonderful girl named Katchie who is an internationally known yoga instructor. She is one of the best on the circuit. The two of them are in the process of moving to Santa Fe to the property owned by Matt and Sarah. Could it get any better than that? I am just so happy that Matt and Josh became good friends. That goes for all my kids . . . all three of them.

Wait . . . what?! you're probably thinking. The math so far shows that Peter only has two kids.

Well, you're not alone. That's the number I had in mind, at least during my first forty years. But then the biggest bombshell of my life hit me:

I got a letter.

That earth-shattering epistle was from a woman, a thirty-three-year-old married, mother of two from Claremont, California. Her name was Christi Linn Campbell McBride. I naturally assumed it was an autograph request. But when I opened the letter, I found out it was a bit more. Christi McBride wrote to me that I was her father, that she was my daughter.

WHOA!!

To say I was stunned would be a gross understatement. To say that I then figured it must be a scam would be totally reasonable. I knew that celebrities were often the target of aberrant fans who imagined they were closer to the stars than they really were. And even more common were the con-men out there looking to profit in some way by establishing a relationship with the celeb. I disregarded the letter. Fortunately, Christi didn't disregard me. More letters followed.

With son Josh and his wife Katchie.

My skepticism held on. I just didn't believe her at first; there was no way I could be her father . . . was there? After all, I had known nothing about her for thirty-three years. How could that even happen? I allowed for the possibility, although I was still pretty sure there had been a mistake.

Christi was so eloquent in her letters, so kind and thoughtful. She made it clear that she didn't want anything from me, no money, no fame by association, no prestige of any sort. There was no anger toward the man who, she may have surmised, had given her away without so much as a second thought. There was none of that. She just wanted to know me, just wanted to know if we could have a relationship, any kind of relationship no matter how small. I began to weaken, but still I resisted meeting her.

The first cracks in my wall of denial came when I got a phone call from Christi's husband, David McBride. He was polite, yet very insistent, saying I just had to at least meet his wife, and then any decision I'd make would be fine with them. I said I'd consider it, then hung up. My mind spun off in a thousand directions, considering every possibility about this being true or not, pondering that if it was true, what had I missed out on in the previous thirty-three years. I ran it by my wife Mary, but ultimately it was my decision to make.

The turning point was a last gasp, Hail Mary, four-page letter from Christi with pictures of Stephanie and Patrick . . . her kids . . . my grandkids.

That did it for me.

It just about broke my heart. It also opened my eyes. I immediately wrote back to her, agreeing to speak to her over the phone. She called two or three times; she was so easy to talk to. Finally, we decided: we were going to get together. I had to see this woman for myself.

We decided to meet at a restaurant. I was at the beach at the time. On the big night, I was early, as usual. I got us a nice, private table in the back of the restaurant and then I waited . . . and waited. It wasn't that long, but to me, the seconds seemed like hours. Husband David came in first, like he was on a reconnaissance mission. He spotted me almost right away, introduced himself, and then sat down to chat for a bit. I'm sure he just wanted to make sure that everything was all right. It was, especially when shortly thereafter, Christi came in. At that instant, my world, my life, my entire being went off in a new direction.

I knew right away she was mine.

It was a wonderful, albeit shocking moment for me, a feeling the likes of which I had never before experienced nor have never felt since. It's impossible to know how people are going to react in a moment like this; for my part, I was pretty much speechless. As Christi spoke, I was mesmerized by her eyes. In them, I could see

With daughter Christi.

me, I could see my mom. There was absolutely no doubt any more.

In a "duh" moment, I quickly realized that my family had not just increased by two, but by double that amount as Christi and David proudly told me about their two kids, Stephanie and Patrick. Yes, I was a grandfather again . . . actually "twice" again!

It turned out that Christi had felt the need to connect with her birth parents in recent years. Her birth mother had given her up for adoption when she was just a few days old. This wonderful young girl had been raised so well by her adoptive parents that there was no reason she had to find us. There was always the chance that her birth parents might not want to meet her, hard as that is for me to imagine.

On the other hand, growing up adopted, there were ample opportunities for her to develop a resentment toward her birth parents for abandoning her. But that was never how she approached it. She just wanted to know. And it was important to me to let her know, and I'm positive about this, that if I had known about her existence, I would have been there for her, one way or another, from day one. But none of that seemed important to her. Thirty-three years of a relationship had been lost for me, for us. But, especially in this case, "late" was definitely better than "never."

I learned Christi had met her future husband David on a Baja cruise; they were married in 1989. David was instrumental in Christi and me finding each other. He was always so supportive of whatever she wanted to do, always encouraging. Christi had used the help of an organization that was dedicated to assisting adopted children reconnect with their birth parents. But in her doing so, word somehow leaked out that she was the daughter of a longtime TV star (that would be me) and *Playboy* magazine's January, 1962, Playmate of the month Merle Pertile.

This was exactly the kind of situation ripe for the inquisitive nosiness of modern TV. I found out Christi had been approached by representatives of both Oprah Winfrey and Phil Donahue. They had each wanted to do a show about her "plight"; but she just turned them down flat. It was not what she was after. Christi just wanted to know her father. Yes, she was definitely my girl.

To this day, I'm still confused as to why Merle didn't let me know she was pregnant. We had dated briefly, but not exclusively, in 1960 when I was between wives one and two. I have no memory of our breakup or even if there was one. Christi had developed a relationship with her birth mother for about four years; she also had the opportunity to talk to Hef about her mother. Ultimately, what was said between mother and daughter remains there. I don't know if Merle's reason for concealing her pregnancy was her career, her beliefs, or some family situation. When Merle took sick, I had a chance to at least see her in the hospital and bring some semblance of closure to the why's and how's of our limited relationship. She passed away in 1997 of complications from heart surgery.

Grandson and granddaughter Patrick and Stephanie McBride.

From the time we first met at the restaurant, Christi and my connection grew, slowly at first, but it was definitely there. For the first year, we both kept our options open. Occasionally, she and her family would come out to the ranch and stay a week or so. We had a tennis court there, and the jacuzzi got quite a workout. And they had a very nice home which I was invited to visit on weekends; I spent a lot of time playing with Stephanie and Patrick in their big backyard. Those kids, my grandkids, have grown up to be incredible young people.

Granddaughter Stephanie has just graduated from Grand Canyon University here in Phoenix not that far from where we live. It was nice being able to see her a lot, especially at her games. Steph is an incredible volleyball player. In high school, she was Newbury Park (California) High School's 2007 MVP and was first team

175

all-conference. In college, she was named to the NCAA Division II West Region Volleyball All-Star second team after ranking fifteenth nationally in blocks. I'm sure she gets her volleyball skills from me (You think?)

Grandson Patrick's sport is basketball. He's currently on the team at San Diego Christian College. I'm bustin' my buttons I'm just so proud of these two.

The revelation of the Browns having a new family member was wonderful news for the rest of the family. Do you remember earlier in this chapter when I mentioned the really big week son Matt had in 1994, that he had not only just been informed by his mother that she was getting a divorce, but that he had also received the letter from his brother concerning Josh's desire to reconnect with the family?

Well, these things always come in three's, don't they? During this same week, the postman brought Matt another letter, this one from me telling him that he now, at the age of twenty-nine, had an older sister. That was the other piece of family business that shook up the Brown family dynamics. For Matt, it was joyous news.

"Oh my god, I have a sister!" he blurted out upon reading my letter.

Matt was surprised, and yet, not surprised. Living in a dysfunctional family that broke up when he was only three and then continued to break up over the years, both on his mom and dad's sides, the thought of a new family member added, not taken away, was very exciting for him. It was a new family.

Matt and Christi get along famously. He thinks she looks a lot like grandmother Mina, my mom, only younger of course. Matt and Christi laugh at a lot of the same things, and they're both very verbal and quite passionate. It's so nice that they love each other, even though as siblings without thirty years of growing up together, they don't have a lot of common stories to fall back upon. Their relationship is just excellent which thrills me to no end. They talk every couple of months and their families see each other about once a year. Granddaughter Stephanie is even coming out to visit her uncle and his family for a week this year.

It's just so great when they all get together. The fact that they grew up in completely different families in different situations allows them not to dwell on the past. Instead, they have great fun discovering each other, focusing more on laughing, sports, and pool time. I wouldn't have it any other way.

Christi and David are now empty-nesters. Where has the time gone? They live in a wonderful house in Newbury Park. KK and I were so touched when, upon deciding to get married in 2008, Christi and David suggested we use their home and huge backyard for our ceremony and reception. It worked out beautifully. We've seen them the most in the last eight years when my career slowed down. Mind you, I said "slowed down," not "was over."

My relationships with my adult children have never been better. I feel that the most important thing a parent can give a kid, especially in a family with the "unusual" history we have, is unconditional love, and I like to think I'm pretty good at it. These relationships are so important. I'm pretty detached from material things. I often hear myself saying, "You like it? Here, have it." What matters to me is my family, each and every one of them. My idea of the perfect time is getting together with them and keeping it very low key. Maybe we'll catch a movie or go on a hike and then sit around and tell stories. I've got all the time in the world for that.

At least, that is, until I become a great-grandfather.

"The more you learn,
the more you learn there's more to learn."
— Frances "Mother" Calvert

Chapter 8
The Metaphysical

My beliefs are pretty much who I am. I believe in being extremely organized; in preparing intensely for every role, on-stage or off; in staying in extraordinary physical condition in order to be ready for all the lefts and rights life throws at you; and, this is the main tenet of my life, I believe in all manner of positive thinking. The polar opposite of that just doesn't work.

Toiling in a field where notoriety, good or bad, is the currency of the realm, I battled mightily to stay on the positive side of public opinion. Even after experiencing four divorces, I still managed to remain civil and private with my personal matters. I like to think I was never responsible for any scandal or outrageous behavior. Nasty gossip rarely attached itself to me. I was never arrested, so there wasn't ever any reason to write outlandish things about me in the fan mags. Positive thinking! It just worked for me.

A good example of my ability to always look for the silver lining, even as a somewhat immature young man (somewhat?), was during my time in the army. As I mentioned before, the general in charge of my base wanted nothing to do with my idea for a theater on the post. Try as I might to convince him, it was a "no-go." An ordinary army private thinking ordinary thoughts would have let it go and moved on to something else. But my perpetual "can-do" attitude wouldn't allow me to let it slide. I figured out the only person who outranked the general in camp was . . . his wife, so to speak. Once I had her sold on the idea of theatre in the cold and wilds of Alaska, I had my theater. Thus the power of positive thinking.

All my life, I've been committed to studying and reading about the metaphysical. I can't remember a time when it wasn't a part of my life. *Webster* defines metaphysical as "beyond the physical or material; incorporeal, supernatural, or transcendental." I didn't understand that definition in my younger years, but I knew it was something in which I needed to become better versed.

Over the years, I've come to appreciate the power of the mind even more so than just being a "positive thinker." Wise people have given me incredible insights. Centers of learning, such as the East Indian metaphysical "Bodhi Tree Bookstore" in Hollywood, have allowed me to immerse myself in literature while meeting people with like interests. I just love to sit down at a table there and soak up the atmosphere. I've also been exposed to some amazing wonders of nature, such as the vortexes of Sedona, Arizona, which have allowed me to absorb their mystical energies during long, lone periods of meditation.

In metaphysics, a common misconception is that you're there just to stimulate your mind. But the whole concept is more; working your mind is great, but you have to remember: your body *IS* your vessel. The more you work on your vessel, the more open you are to receive new information, experiences, and messages. You need to keep the body fit in order to keep the mind fit, pure, and open. I know that now, but it took me a few years before I learned the real value of a body in shape. From a more practical viewpoint, staying fit was part of my job. In essence, I was selling my body to the viewing public.

I had always participated in a myriad of sports in my youth, but

I was never serious about keeping myself fit until I got my first big job in television. *Lawman's* star, John Russell, was my inspiration for perspiration. Former Marine John knew the value of exercise and he was determined to make me a devotee of the sweat-set. I became his protégé, his workout buddy. We skipped lunch almost every day during *Lawman* shooting, opting for our private workout facility over the Warner Brothers' cafeteria.

Workout facility. It probably sounds nicer than it was, but it was quite functional for us. Our private "gym" was an unused building on the Warner Brothers' back lot; together, we turned it into a fitness center with no monthly dues. John brought in a stationary bike and we had weights all over the place. He then proceeded to put me through a regimen of exercises that pain me to this day just thinking about them. Nevertheless, it worked. It took me a few weeks, but I actually came to look forward to my time in the "gym." Not just satisfied with sculpting the external me, John also worked on the inner me, adding to my diet a powdered liquid concoction he called "Tigers' Milk."

"Here's your lunch," he'd say handing me a big jug of the stuff. That happened every day, and every day he'd watch me with those steely eyes to ensure I downed every drop. I usually did. And although my time with John on *Lawman* eventually ended in 1962, my workouts did not. Amazingly, they had become a part of me and still are, in one form or another, to this day. I currently weigh in at 173 pounds, close to what I was back then fifty years ago. My workouts have served me well.

The older I got, the more I searched for greater self-awareness and inner peace. I tried a lot of things: meditation, the study of Oriental philosophies, metaphysics, and other roads to enlightenment. Dr. Ross McLean, whom I'll speak more of later in this chapter, gave me one of my prized possessions: a copy of the Hindu bible called *Bhagavad Gita*; "Gita" means "song." In it, there are

700 verses covering everything. I've read and re-read it cover-to-cover many times.

I learned the most about meditation when I joined a study group chaired by the esteemed philosophy teacher Frances "Mother" Calvert. We would meet weekly in Long Beach, California, which was a bit of a haul for me. It didn't matter. I managed to drive there every weekend just to be a part of her class. It was incredible how much her teachings helped to expand my mind. I really learned to think there. I always remember a phrase she often uttered: "The more you learn, the more you learn there's more to learn."

I was not limited to expanding my thought horizons just on weekends. Back in the city, I had slowly accumulated a group of friends whose idea of a good time was sitting around my living room with a cup of coffee and discussing the meaning of love. I had incredible talks with these people, and soon word of our conversations spread. These casual get-togethers became so encompassing, the topics about love and its many facets so intriguing, that I decided to formalize the group so that like-minded people could get together to hammer things out no matter what those "things" were in a series of deep, philosophical discussions. It became a real spiritual undertaking. "S.O.L." or the "Study of Love" brought my loosely knit group of people together weekly at my house for the actual study of love. It sounds so sixtyish now when I say it, but there were concepts and ideas brought forth that stayed with me for the rest of my life. And of course, "Sol" also references the sun, a tremendous source of energy and enlightenment. So there's that, too.

These meetings would last a couple of hours; I lucked out when I was able to get Mother Calvert as our spiritual teacher. She orchestrated the meetings, keeping us on point and making sure everyone was heard. One of her favorite things was to talk about spiritual energy. She brought this concept home to all of us one night in a most extraordinary way. To this day, I can not explain it.

It had gotten pretty late one night when suddenly Mother stopped the conversation by holding up one hand.

"Excuse me," she said. She then got up, went to my back door, and walked out into my yard in the pitch-black of the night. Confused, we all followed to see where she was going and what she was doing. Suddenly and with no warning, the entire backyard came alive with light; it was totally illuminated. We stood there transfixed; it was as bright as day out there, yet the clock had just struck one a.m. There were no obvious sources of the light, just Mother standing there looking up with her arms raised. Our immediate responses were to "ooh" and "ahh," but then one and soon others began to question what they had seen, what was actually happening, and how it was possible. They wanted to know what the "trick" was.

Oh, ye of little faith, I thought.

I smiled to myself. I didn't need an explanation. I knew. The light came from her.

Our discussion meetings were not meant to turn us into a psychoanalytical therapy group. We would talk about general concepts usually, but not always, related to love. I tried not to let it become too big so that everyone would have the amount of time they needed to fully participate, to speak and be heard. On a more practical level, my house was limited in size. I had to make a rule that friends were not allowed to bring friends. Participants had to be someone with whom I had not only conversed, but that I felt possessed the right conception of what S.O.L. was all about.

S.O.L. began when I was between wives. My time was definitely freed up then. But as with all good things, it eventually had to come to an end. We just grew too large, had too many interested people. While that would seem to be a great problem to have for most groups, for us it had become far too unwieldy. The problem resolved itself when I moved away, although I continued to study with Mother right up until her death.

It's funny, but you'd think that intense introspection such as we were committed to in these sessions would have helped my marriages. My wives and I were certainly forward-thinking enough that it was never a case of where one of us had to agree with the other. It was, to each of us, our own personal spirituality. Unfortunately, at least up until the present with KK, my wives never seemed to understand this part of me.

My quest for spiritual knowledge achieved in a group dynamic did not end with S.O.L. I later spent over a year in Santa Monica studying with the world-renowned Swami Muktananda, an Indian Hindu guru and disciple of Bhagavan Nityananda. The Swami, also known less formally as "Baba Gee" to his faithful, had quite the following, one that would definitely NOT have fit in my living room. He hosted weekly meetings at the Santa Monica Civic Auditorium where the seating capacity was 3,000. Swami Muktananda was the founder of "Siddha Yoga," a spiritual path based on the Hindu spiritual traditions of Kashmir Shaivism. I learned Siddha Yoga from him, often sitting and meditating while doing it. I was even quoted in *Soap Opera Digest* about my studies with Baba Gee, saying, "I call it 'self-realization' and I've gained a lot from it."

Baba Gee has also written a number of books on the subjects of Kundalini Shakti and Vedanta as well as the aforementioned Kashmir Shaivism. His teachings can best be summarized by two of his quotations:

1) Honor, worship, and meditate on your self; and
2) God dwells within you as you; see God in each other.

I truly believe these quotes and their inherent accuracy. I've studied a lot of different philosophies for a number of years, but I always come back to these two sayings by the Swami.

Baba Gee held his meetings for a multitude of people. I went every week for more than a year. I once had my car stolen while attending one of these meetings, but I kept believing in the power of positive thinking while meditating on his weekly teachings. Soon enough, I got my car back.

I wasn't the only "celebrity" attending these meetings. Through Baba Gee, I met John Denver. I just happened to be in the front row one Saturday when Denver was there to entertain the congregation. He asked if there were any requests, so typical me, I blurted out, "*Boy From the Country!*" John recognized me and began laughing at my outspokenness. We had a nice conversation after that day's talk.

Baba Gee's meetings fell somewhere between a lecture and a seminar. He didn't know much English, so he had a woman, Chid Villa Sonanda, interpret for him. He spoke to all people; every walk of life was represented at these meetings, and every person was touched, each in his or her unique way.

This one's a little weird. The last time I saw Baba Gee speak, he announced that he would be leaving his earthly existence soon, actually citing October 2nd as the exact day he would pass away. I soon heard he had flown back to his native India. Sure enough, on October 2, 1982, the precise day he had predicted for his death, Baba Gee passed on to the next world. Incredibly, he had taken the mystery out of dying. He had not been diagnosed with any life threatening disease, nor had he died under questionable circumstances. He simply had the will and desire to move on to his next plane of existence.

A shrine was built at the end of the Pacific Coast highway in Pacific Palisades, California, to commemorate Swami Muktananda. It's not dogmatic at all, nor does it espouse any particular religion. The "Lake Shrine" is a terrifically beautiful, dedicated structure in a most bucolic setting. I continue to find it fascinating. It expands you. Whenever I'm in southern California, I make a point of spending time there. It's wonderful to walk the path around the lake and find one of the many intimate places to sit and quietly contemplate life. There have been times when I've arrived at 10 a.m. and am still there at 4 p.m. That always surprises me that the time flies by so fast. It's just that the park is so freeing.

The sixties and early seventies were a time of great upheaval in our society, and the rebellious part of our nation was doing many things to alter and expand their minds, going diametrically away from the conventions of their parents. Instead of mind-numbing alcohol, they chose to investigate their total consciousness through the use of alternative drugs. I was never much of a drinker and was certainly not close to abusing drugs of any kind. Marlboro cigarettes were about as druggy as I got in those years. The funny thing was, *Lawman* was sponsored by Camel, but they were a little too intense for me being unfiltered and all. They used to give each of us on the show a carton a week, but since I had recently quit smoking, I gave them to John Russell. In hindsight, it's a bit oxymoronic now to think of the incredibly fit star of *Lawman* smoking Camel unfiltereds, but in those days, it seemed like everybody, especially in Hollywood, smoked. Of course, my smoking wasn't just limited to tobacco. Like most young people of that era, I also indulged occasionally in the use of marijuana in social settings. Hard drugs were definitely not my thing.

My lone foray into the world of illegal pharmaceuticals was all part of a desire to seek ever growing knowledge through the expansion of my mind. To aid in that quest, I figured it was time for me to try Lysergic acid diethylamide . . . better known as "LSD."

I knew of a doctor in Canada, Ross McLean, who was the head of a private hospital outside Vancouver. Good things were being said about Dr. McLean. It was well known that he had helped the legendary actor Cary Grant resolve some personal issues through the use of LSD. Dr. McLean administered therapeutic sessions with LSD in a controlled environment, an idea that both intrigued and excited me. At that time, I was in an extremely investigative mode.

If there are things for me to learn, I thought, *I want to learn them.*

Except for terminally ill cancer patients, LSD was illegal in the United States. However, that was not the case in Canada. That's where I planned to go for my experiment. I made an appointment with the good doctor's office, then flew to Vancouver. I actually stayed at the house where Dr. McLean and his wife Isabella lived. They were very pleasant, introspective people; we had a big discussion at dinner that evening about the aspects of what I would be experiencing the next day. Our discourse carried over well into the night.

The next day, we went to his office. There was a big lounge chair into which I comfortably settled. I had to take off all jewelry and anything else that was binding against my skin. He then gave me what looked to be a plain glass of water. I drank it down willingly, then relaxed back into the overstuffed chair.

It didn't take long for the LSD to do its job. I began to hallucinate wildly, vivid colors flashing through my mind while all sorts of mixed images danced to the forefront. It was exhausting, yet turbulently invigorating, frantic yet somehow calming. Go figure. The thoughts and images, totally new to my experience, raced through my mind. I should have taken notes, although that certainly wasn't possible for my then current frame of mind.

What I learned from this amazing experience was that LSD enhances your ability to be more a part of what is around you. It opens your mind to the fact that there is a lot more going on than of what you may be aware. And for all the hallucinating that was occurring, I felt amazingly at ease. In the end, the LSD's calming effect took over. My sensitivities were enhanced, yet I had no fear. I kept looking forward to what the next part of the experience would be. Later, we took a drive out to Dr. McLean's ranch. There, I got on a horse while still under the influence. I had been on a lot of horses in my lifetime, but I never had a ride like that one.

A year later, I went back for more of the same. This time it was better, if such a thing was even possible. Any apprehensions I had during the previous year's experiment were completely gone in this go-around. A major influence I picked up from my exposure to this most misunderstood drug the second time around was how it enhanced my ability to meditate. Meditation had become a huge part of my life, so anything that could make it better was an enormous benefit for me. It was a learning experience that would help me in all walks of my life.

I never experienced LSD again. I certainly would have never used the drug by myself. Having Dr. McLean there to guide me through those most unusual trips was the only way to go.

As is usually perceived of that era, drugs such as LSD were often paired with the sexual mores of the time, and I was definitely a card-carrying soldier in the battle of the sexes. The sexual revolution was kind of my life, although I always acted carefully and respectfully with women. I definitely believed in the Golden Rule: do unto others as you would have them do unto you. This guiding principle was and is a major influence on my life.

The Golden Rule in one form or another is a major doctrine of all the world's great religions. My belief in the same allowed me not to be tied to any one particular religion in order to practice this way of life. In essence, I was never mean to anybody.

Actual organized religion was never a big part of my family life. My parents were not religious; they both had some basic Catholic training but nothing fanatical. Growing up, I was never coerced to obey the tenets of any organized religion. My mother was an actress, so she could become a character who could talk about it, but it was never something she truly felt. And strangely enough, none of my wives were religious either; none of them ever tried to convert me to any way of thinking theologically. What are the odds?

I just could never accept the idea of organized religion, of somebody telling you what to do or what to believe. I never found an organized religion that kept in step with my logical mind. That makes it difficult to put a label on exactly what it is I do believe. I definitely like the idea that there's at least one religion out there that works. It's just that I haven't found it yet. So in the meanwhile during times of conflict, I simply default to The Golden Rule.

It works for me.

"I guess I was paying her too much."
— Sammy Davis Jr., on hearing his housekeeper
had just purchased a hotel

Chapter 9

Sammy, Dean & Frank: The Rat Pack

I was fortunate enough to have been a small, very small part of the legendary "Rat Pack" of the 1960s. I can use the term "Rat Pack" now since all of the members of that illustrious group have made it on up to that big stage in the sky, but if they knew I was writing this using, as Frank would put it, "that stupid phrase," I'm sure they'd be back in a second to whomp me upside the head.

The term "Rat Pack" was mainly used by the press and the public. None of the guys ever referred to themselves as that; instead, they preferred "The Summit." Initially, Frank liked calling the group "The Clan," but it would be hard to imagine Sammy Davis Jr. as a part of any group going by a name which included the word "Clan," regardless of whether or not it was spelled with a "C" or a "K." Sammy convinced Frank to go with "The Summit" to avoid having people think there was any connection at all with "the Ku Klux Klan."

Segregation was still prevalent in this country then, but the Rat Pack boys would have nothing to do with it. They wouldn't entertain at any Vegas casino that still endorsed segregationist policies. And given the fact that they were so hugely popular and sold just an absolutely humongous number of tickets, Las Vegas hotels either had to change their policies or else risk losing their most popular entertainers. Oh, it wasn't that the casino owners didn't see colors; they did . . . green. The segregationist policies changed quickly.

Most people are unaware that the Frank-Dean-Sammy pairing was not the first incarnation of "The Rat Pack." That honor goes to Humphrey Bogart and Lauren Bacall back in the fifties. As I've heard it told, Bogart was the leader of a group of serious carousers who included Errol Flynn, Spencer Tracy, Cary Grant, Judy Garland, and a youngish Frank Sinatra among others. On one trip back to the group's headquarters which doubled as a home for Bogie and Bacall, Lauren took one look at the bedraggled, inebriated group of partyers and ceremoniously announced, "You guys look like a goddamned rat pack." The name apparently stuck.

My association with "The Summit" stemmed from my friendship with Sammy Davis Jr. My initial acquaintance with the most talented man I ever met eventually led to my playing tennis at Dean's house, drinking with Frank in Hollywood, and even being pulled up on stage in Las Vegas at the Sands Hotel as a sort of Rat Pack team mascot. In hindsight, Shirley MacLaine, Angie Dickinson, and Marilyn Monroe, considerably more famous than me, were known as the actual "Rat Pack Mascots." But I was just happy to be part of the group in any way I could. Peter Lawford and Joey Bishop were other Summit members, but Sammy, Dean, and Frank were the ones I knew best. Ah, those were times I'll never forget.

Frank Sinatra, the Chairman of the Board himself, was an incredibly nice man, despite what you may have heard. Oh sure, he was tough when he had to be, but he was always so much fun to be around. A tad intimidating, perhaps, but he was not scary in the least.

I remember once walking into the Polo Lounge, a club inside the Beverly Hills Hotel. As I headed to the bar, I heard someone call out.

"Hey! Kid! Over here!"

It took my eyes a moment to adjust to the dimly lit room.

"John Wayne!" the voice called out again. "Get your butt over here!"

I turned to where the voice was coming from. There in a huge corner booth sat Frank, Sammy, and a few other friends laughing uproariously. Cocktail glasses smothered the top of their table. I wandered over tentatively, still unsure of exactly where I stood with "Old Blue Eyes."

"Sit down!" Frank ordered.

When the Boss says "Sit down!", you sit down, no matter if it's a chair, a stool, or on the floor. Frank slid over to make room for me.

This was pretty heady stuff for a young actor in his twenties. The guys all treated me like we'd been friends for years. I sat there listening, only speaking when spoken to, as the table's conversation stampeded onwards in many different directions.

Soon enough, a waiter came over with a telephone and plugged it in near our table. This was in the days before cell phones. Somehow, I just can't imagine Frank as a cell phone guy. Anyway, the call was for Frank, of course. It was a business call, so he took it at the table while the rest of us just kept yakking away. There were at least three conversations going on, but it didn't seem to bother Frank.

Now into the eye of this celebrity storm came an autograph hound, pen and signature book in hand and no fear in his eyes. Either not caring that Frank was on the phone or else just being totally oblivious, he shoved his pen and book at Frank. I waited for the inevitable verbal onslaught to be rained down upon this man.

"Hey, Sinatra! Can you sign this?"

The rest of the table's gossip came to a screeching halt. Frank put his eyes on the guy, all the while not missing a word of his phone conversation.

"Come on, you can sign this."

The interloper was nothing if not persistent. Frank nodded as he held up his hand, saying without saying that he'd be with him in a minute. That, however, wasn't good enough for this guy.

Frank kept talking and the guy kept interrupting. It was as if none of the rest of us even existed. The bull kept charging and matador Frank kept parrying.

Finally, he pushed his autograph book just a bit too close to Frank's face. You could see in his eyes that Frank had definitely had enough. On what would be the guy's final thrust, Frank took the phone handset and whacked him hard on the hand. It was like he had just swatted a fly.

The table exploded in laughter. It was nothing too physical, nothing got hurt except for maybe the boor's feelings, but it definitely sent a message: Mind your manners around Frank.

The guy was pissed, but there wasn't anything he could do. Off he slithered into the darkness of the room.

There weren't many people in the bar that day, but there must have been at least one with big ears and a loose tongue. Sure enough, the next day in Variety, the headlines read: "SINATRA ATTACKS INNOCENT BYSTANDER."

Can you believe that?! Frank's reputation had preceded him again. I had witnessed the entire exchange, seen the exact circumstances of the "attack." Any one of you would have reacted in the same way. The use of the word "attack" was totally inaccurate and misleading, not an unusual trick in those days for the Hollywood press. But that's life when you were a public figure as big as Frank. As he later said, "Ah, what the fuck are you going to do?"

The print and broadcast media could, and can still be, ruthless when it came to celebrities and their fame. Depending upon which reporter or columnist you were dealing with, your career might be headed for a rocky stretch if one of those guys had it in for you, to hell with the facts. I had also been the victim of a misrepresented article, although mine didn't even have a nodding acquaintance with the truth. This time, it was *The Los Angeles Herald Examiner.*

An egotistical gossip columnist named Harrison Carroll somehow got the mistaken idea that I had been out at a very public spot canoodling with Miss California, Teri Janssen. The blurb read: *Lawman* star Peter Brown was seen last night at Dan Tanna's Restaurant on Melrose presenting Miss California with a present."

The problem with this was twofold: 1) I had a girlfriend at the time; and 2) I had never met Teri Janssen in my life.

That article had the potential to screw up everything for me, so I called and demanded a retraction. A very pompous copy editor claimed there was nothing he could do, but I was persistent. I called his boss and then his boss's boss and so on, all the way up the food chain. When nothing happened, I got a hold of Carroll and threatened other actions, both legal and marginally less so. I was one determined boyfriend.

Finally, they printed a retraction, probably just to get rid of me. I breathed a sigh of relief. The proof of my innocence, right there in black-and-white, gave life to the relationship between my lady friend and me . . . at least for awhile. On the plus side, having gotten to know Harrison a bit, I later went back to him and asked for an introduction to Teri. And wonder upon wonders, he agreed to introduce us. Even those gossip creeps have a heart sometimes. It was the first time a misquote ever paid off for me. We ended up dating for a short time . . . Teri, that is, not Harrison. Can't be too careful now, can you?

Another member of the Rat Pack was almost as notorious as Frank, only instead of being known for his anger, Dean Martin was viewed as a bon vivant with an incredible lust for liquor. And as with Frank, his public image was far from what he was like in real life.

Now, just as it has helped me so many other times in my life, so did the game of tennis indirectly get me introduced to Dean. I actually got to know him through his son, Dean Paul (also known as "Dino" during his teen years). I began playing tennis with Dean Paul during my run on *Laredo*. At the time, I thought I was good, but this kid could bring it. He ran me all over the court. Of course, he was about fifteen years younger than me, but I hesitate to use that as an excuse. He was actually good enough to qualify for and play in the junior competition at Wimbledon, and later competed against many pros in exhibitions around the country.

When I say this guy could "bring it," I'm not just talking about tennis. As a singer in the group "Dino, Desi and Billy," he had several big songs, twice landing them on the top thirty charts. As an actor, he had a Golden Globe movie nomination and later starred in the television show, *Misfits of Science*. And beyond the world of show business and sports, he was also a tremendous pilot, getting his license at the tender age of sixteen. He went on to fly jets for the California Air National Guard while attaining the rank of captain.

I was competitive enough with Dean Paul that we began to have a regular tennis game. And of course through him, I eventually met his father, the legendary Dean Martin.

"Come on over to the house," Dean said. "I have a court."

That was all I needed. Through tennis, I became a regular at Dean's Beverly Hills home at 601 Mountain Drive just off Sunset Boulevard. Playing there often, I got to know the whole family, including Dean's wife Jeanne, a fine tennis player herself. And when you were at the Martin's, you never knew who you'd encounter in the kitchen or on the court: Ruthie Berle (Uncle Miltie's wife and Jeanne's best friend), Janet Leigh, Gene Kelly, just to name a few. We all became good friends. I was especially happy to meet Gene Kelly, and it was a real thrill to play tennis with him. I was so excited to get to know a star of his caliber. He was such a beautiful man and, I might add, a very good tennis player.

In all the years I played there, however, I never knew Dean

to pick up a racquet. A bottle, perhaps; a glass, quite likely; but a racquet, never. While Jeanne and Dean Paul's friends played, Dean would hang around his bar where he had a perfect view of the court. He'd watch us for hours at a time. Little did I know that this particular bar which symbolized so much of the Dean Martin persona would, in a few short years, be mine.

At that time, I had just bought a house from my agent, Sy Marsh. On a particularly bright and warm Sunday morning, I had gone over to the Martins' for a game of tennis. As I made my way through their massive home, I noticed that the L-shaped bar at which Dean had spent so much time had been ripped away from the wall, leaving its torn imprint on the wallpaper behind it. It was just sitting there, so sad, so forlorn, like an untethered ship without its captain.

"So, what are you going to do with that old bar?" I asked Dean as he entered the room.

"This ancient thing?" he replied. "Why? You want it?"

Surprised at the offer, I fumbled for an answer.

"Well . . . sure."

I definitely had enough room for it in my new house; there was hardly a stick of furniture in the place. There were any of a number of locations it would fit. In a pinch, it could even double as my dining room table. Just don't ask me how I figured that out.

"I tell you what I'll do," he said after thinking for a moment. "If you can get this pile of kindling out of here, I'll give it to you."

"You've got a deal!" I blurted out, not waiting to think of the problems inherent with transporting a heavy, giant, oak bar with a clunky fold-down leaf. I was too taken with the possibility of owning Dean Martin's bar.

Think of the stories I could tell, my thought process went. *I can own Dean Martin's bar! That's going to be incredible! It'll be like owning one of Rod Laver's tennis racquets.*

I settled down long enough to call Dick Davis, a buddy in the clothing business who, along with John and Don Ellis, were partners with me in the ownership of a twenty-six-foot Chris-Craft boat. Dick was the only person I knew who owned a pickup truck. Pretty much everybody else in my Hollywood crowd had little, two-seater convertibles or fancy Mercedes. A pickup truck was the only way I was going to be able to transport this massive piece of saloon furniture to my swinging new bachelor pad. Dick and I struggled mightily, scraping more than a few knuckles along the way, but we finally got it into my new house where it proudly stood for many years and was the source of oh-so many wonderful stories during that time.

It's a bit off-topic, but my mention of Dick Davis reminds me of a great story. We had kept our boat at Marina del Rey so it would be convenient for our many trips to Catalina Island, "twenty-six miles across the sea." Sometimes, however, we used it to go shark hunting. Yes, that's right: shark hunting.

Early in the morning, we'd head out a short way into the Pacific Ocean. We'd slow almost to a stop, then haul out a metal ramp on the bow of the boat, our "gang plank" so to speak, where we would stand poised at the ready with our trusty harpoon. The "harpoon" was really just a spear we had fashioned with a detachable barb connected to a 100' cable.

Early morning was good because the sharks liked to hang out just below the surface and enjoy the warmth of the sun. When we'd come upon one, Dick or I would toss the harpoon at the unfortunate creature. Tied to the other end of the cable was an inflated inner tube. If we were fortunate enough to spear the shark, it would swim away, but the dragging of the inner tube behind it eventually would cause him to run out of steam. That's how they did it in *Jaws* years later so . . .

Hey! It just dawned on me! Spielberg stole our idea!

O.K., so anyway, after the shark tired, the two of us would pull him in, carefully. Then we'd dock the boat and take the shark, or sharks, to some local restaurants. They'd always be delighted to see us. And the money we'd receive for these vicious delicacies would pay for the rest of the day's crucial liquids, i.e., gas for the boat, oil for the engine, cocktails for the sailors. You get my drift.

O.K., I got off-track. I stayed close to Dean's family and, in doing so, learned a lot about the human condition. One day the doorbell rang; Dean asked me to answer it. When I opened the door, I was surprised to see a bunch of tourists complete with black socks and sandals and the obligatory camera hanging around each neck. They had as much nerve as Frank's autograph seeker at the Polo Lounge, and they, too, wanted an autograph . . . Dean's autograph, not mine.

I was just about to tell the intruders to shove off when from behind me I heard, "I got this."

It was Dean.

To my surprise, he walked out onto the front steps and treated the insensitive tourists like long-lost family. There were a lot of laughs as he took the time, while using his great sense of humor, to give each one of them an autograph and a great memory. That one small act of kindness taught me a lot about how a star should treat his fans. I've always remembered that.

When I got married to Yvette, my third wife, in 1971, we had a small ceremony in Beverly Hills. Both Sammy and Dean were there. Well, just before I was to utter those two fateful words, "I do," the sound of snoring rang out through the church. Yes, there in one of the front pews was Dean, sound asleep . . . and snoring to beat the band. Sammy, sitting nearby, was laughing uncontrollably while motioning for people to NOT wake Dean up.

Yeah, those were my buddies.

Dean's life took a horrible turn in 1987 when Dean Paul, flying with the California Air National Guard, took an F4 Phantom fighter jet out on a training mission. It was snowing at the time. I think there was some problem with the altimeter. Whatever it was, the visibility was extremely limited. Dean Paul's plane crashed into the San Bernardino Mountains. He and another officer never had a chance.

I attended Dean Paul's funeral and I've got to tell you there's nothing sadder than the sight of parents burying a child. I tried to speak to Dean, but his eyes were vacant. His son's death absolutely devastated him; he was almost destroyed by it. Dean hung in there for another eight years, but nothing for him was ever really the same. He died on Christmas Day, 1995.

Sammy Davis Jr. was just a kid off the streets of New York, but he became one of the most talented entertainers in the world, equally adept at singing, dancing, and acting. Sammy appeared on two episodes of *Lawman*, although I had previously known him through Sy Marsh at the William Morris Agency.

On our show, Sammy played "Willie Shay," a pleasant enough cowboy who was bullied by others. Besides featuring the talented Davis, the episodes were extra distinctive for the pet Willie kept: "Blue Boss," a huge Guernsey cow.

It's funny that in the four seasons *Lawman* was on the air, we almost always won the ratings war for our time slot; we were in the top ten every year. And in that time, we were mostly up against *The Ed Sullivan Show* during his second half-hour. The only time Ed beat us in the ratings was when he had as his guest . . . that's right, you guessed it: Sammy Davis Jr.

The mind boggles at the sheer number of talents that Sammy possessed. But there was one thing I could do better than him, and he wasn't happy about it. Ever the competitor, he begged me to teach him and that's how Sammy learned to "quick draw."

After his first try at whipping a six-shooter out of a holster, I could see that he was a natural. He definitely planned on becom-

Joking with Sammy Davis Jr.

ing the best and then including it in his act. After several days of practice, he became good . . . quite good. He got so fast that he might have even been better than me, although I would never admit to it . . .

Come to think of it, I guess I just did. Whatever.

The two of us never went head to head, so the question of who was faster did not get answered.

Sammy and I grew to be great friends. We worked together only once more, however, this time in 1967 on *The Danny Thomas Hour*. In a racially electrified script, he and I performed the most intense scene in which I ever participated.

Sammy battled racial discrimination his entire life. His second marriage, this time to the white, Swedish-born actress May Britt, unleashed a torrent of hate unlike anything I had ever seen. It came to a head when Sammy was doing a one-man show at the Huntington Hartford Theater on Vine Street at about the same time that he was about to marry May.

Sammy was backstage getting ready for the show while outside, unbeknownst to him, there were what we would now term "white supremacists" marching in Nazi uniforms holding signs saying "Keep Our Nordic Race Pure." Well, all I can say is thank goodness for Sammy's agent, Steve Blauncr.

Back then, Steve was with the William Morris Agency. He was an incredible man. Sammy often said Steve was, and I quote: " . . . big enough to eat hay and shit in the street."

When they first got to know each other, Steve was in the military and would often go to the Copacabana to see Sammy perform. Blauner idolized Davis. During a break one evening, Steve summoned up the courage to approach Sammy and introduce himself.

His opening line to Sammy was, "The way you feel about Frank Sinatra is the way I feel about you." They soon became fast friends and saw each other often.

After his time in the service, Steve got into the business part

With Sammy, John Russell and Sammy's parents, Elvera Sanchez and Sammy Davis Sr., on *Lawman* set.

of the entertainment world. His versatile career included managing super-singer Bobby Darin as well as working with big names like Richard Pryor, Nat King Cole, George Burns, Jack Nicholson, Perry Como, Peggy Lee, and Pat Boone. The company he later formed made movies such as *Easy Rider, The Last Picture Show,* and *The King of Marvin Gardens.* He was also responsible for the popular television shows *Bewitched, I Dream of Jeannie,* and the offbeat musical youth comedy, *The Monkees.* Steve once told me, "We were trying to sell *The Monkees* to NBC. After showing them the pilot, the lights came on in the screening room. Head of programming Mort Viner just sat there shaking his head before finally sighing loudly.

'I don't know what the hell we've just seen,' he announced, 'but

I think we should put it on the air."'

So much for the science of television evaluation methods.

Back at the Huntington Hartford Theater, Steve wasn't about to allow his friend Sammy to be abused by these racists pigs, especially right there in front of the theater, so he boldly marched up and pulled a sign away from one of them. At that moment, all hell broke loose.

The police came and helped Steve and me deal with the fight that had broken out, although not many of the protesters wanted a piece of the giant man now menacing them. In the end, the police carted away in a paddy wagon the few that were left. Sammy never knew what went on out front.

Although Sammy and I didn't work together anymore, we did see each other socially quite a bit. If you knew Sammy, you were very aware that he loved cars. He once called me to say he was coming over to show me his new ride. A half-hour later, down the street came Sammy in a brand new Rolls Royce. It was something else. Sammy told me to hop in and then off we went to the theater where the Academy Awards were being held. It was also the site for a screening of a movie in which Sammy was appearing. It wasn't that he was so excited about the movie; it was really just that he very much wanted to drive up to that august location in a Rolls Royce.

On a different occasion, Sammy again wanted to show his pride in yet another one of his many vehicles, this time a brand new Thunderbird. I, on the other hand, had recently purchased a used 1958 Mercedes convertible for $2,500. Now, the body was in pretty good shape but the top was shredded and the wooden dashboard, formerly a deep ebony with streaks of blond, was peeled. I have to admit it looked like crap.

I had a friend, a car geek named Larry Watson, who could turn back time on this car and make it appear new. He ordered leather from England for the seats and had it installed. Although the wood had to be taken out, I still needed wheels to get around, so for a few months I drove just the skeleton of the car. I may have looked ridiculous, but I was just biding my time. When it was all done, I knew it had been worth it. Finished with seven coats of candy-apple red paint, it looked like it came right off the showroom floor.

The first thing I did was to call Sammy and tell him I was coming over to take him for a ride. He had no idea what I had done.

From the moment when I drove up, I could see he was thrown for a loop. Ever the fierce competitor, he looked askance at me as he walked around my car giving it a complete inspection. All he could manage to say was a muttered, "Yeah . . . right."

Of course, the next time I saw Sammy, he was grinning at me from behind the wheel of his T-Bird. He had just had it painted . . . and by Larry Watson . . . and, oh that's right, it was . . . Candy-Apple Red!

Over the years, I spent a lot of time at Sammy's house. Just like at Dean's, you never knew who you were going to run into at Sammy's pad. He did have a regular group of buddies we played poker with that included his dad, Tony Curtis, and Mel Torme. Sometimes we'd play at Mel's house, but usually the game was at Sammy's.

Now, Sammy had a pool, but curiously, he couldn't swim. That just didn't do it for his poker buddies. A plan was hatched.

One Sunday morning, the poker boys made a pact. We established a code word, something we all knew Sammy would say. When the inevitable code word was announced, we pounced on Sammy and carried him screaming to the side of his pool. I'm dead sure he didn't believe we'd toss him in.

He was wrong.

SPLASH!

There he was, bobbing up and down, screaming furiously as he flailed away. We had gathered close to the edge of the pool to make sure he didn't drown. Swearing and flailing, flailing and swearing, he finally struggled to the side of the pool.

"YOU COCKSUCKERS!" he screamed.

That only made us laugh even more. Gradually, after wiping water out of his eyes and smoothing his hair back, a smile returned to his face. He couldn't hold it in anymore: giant waves of belly laughs poured forth from this smallish man. And strangely enough, for the rest of the day we couldn't get him out of the pool.

And that's how Sammy Davis's poker buddies taught him to swim.

Sammy did always have a way of turning around any awkward moment. At one of his poker games, it was Tony Curtis's turn to deal. He shuffled the cards several times, then looked around the table.

"O.K., boys, this time . . . " he announced grandly, ". . . .we'll play five-card draw. And just to make it interesting, let's have a wild card." He thought for a moment.

"One-eyed Jews are wild."

Everybody froze at the table . . . total silence. Tony had meant to say "one-eyed jacks," but had misspoken. Nobody knew how Sammy would react to that. He had recently returned from Israel where he had converted to Judaism. And of course due to a traffic accident years ago, he did just have sight in only one eye.

Never one to miss an opportunity to amuse and entertain, quick thinking Sammy immediately took his glass eye out and laid it on the card table right in front of Tony. The star of the legendary film *Some Like It Hot* turned all shades of red. Laughter erupted at the table and, of course, all was well for the rest of the evening.

Speaking of Israel, it once happened that I was making a movie there when I heard Sammy was coming to Tel Aviv and would be staying at the same hotel as me. I knew that Sammy's favorite drink was I.W. Harper Bourbon and Vernor's Ginger Ale, so I scoured the city trying to find some. Unfortunately, there was none to be had anywhere. Ever the resourceful boy that I was, I got a hold of a stewardess who worked the L.A.-Tel Aviv flights and enlisted her help. Sure enough, on her next flight to Tel Aviv, she came to the hotel armed with two bottles, one a Vernor's and the other an I.W. Harper Bourbon.

Sammy was booked into the Presidential Suite. I asked a few questions, pulled a few strings, and was able to find out when he would be arriving. I hired two beautiful Israeli girls and had them stand at attention one on each side of the elevator door leading into the suite. One was wearing a full-dress army uniform, the other a little less formally attired . . . she was topless!

I got into the suite, mixed Sammy's favorite drink, and then waited for the phone to ring. I'd made friends with the hotel's head honcho and had asked him to call me the moment Sammy arrived.

RINNNGGG!

There was my signal that Sammy was on his way up. I listened at the door. Suddenly, I heard his scream, followed by peals of laughter and the sound of him stomping his feet on the floor as he was known to do whenever he got really excited. He had obviously noticed the girls.

Still weak with laughter, he staggered into the room followed by what we would nowadays call "his posse." I advanced directly to Sammy, handing him his drink without saying a word, then headed out of the room.

"Hello, Murf! Howdy, Georgie!" I said to his assistant, Murphy Bennett, and his band leader, George Rhodes. "Hiya, gang!" I exclaimed to the rest of his entourage. I opened the door.

"Brown!" Sammy shouted. "What the hell are you doing here?!"

"I just wanted to make sure you felt at home, " I replied, "so I jetted in ahead of you. Welcome to Israel. Shalom!"

Exit, stage left. As my mom often told me, "Always leave them on a high note."

Sunday mornings at Sammy's had become a ritual for me.

When we had first met, Sammy invited me to a Sunday brunch at his house on Sunset Plaza. There, I was greeted by Alma, his maid/cook/housekeeper. Alma told me Sammy was expecting me and directed me to go down to the pool house. There, I ran into Gene Kelly as well as Warner Brothers vice-president Hugh Benson. Pat Henry, who often opened for Sammy as well as Frank, was sitting poolside talking to Shirley MacLaine. This was some pretty heady company.

When Sammy saw me, he let out a whoop and ran over to to give me a big hug. In front of all these celebrities, most of whom I did not yet know, well, it startled me. I guess I froze up.

Sammy felt it too. Undeterred, he firmly grabbed my shoulders, pulled me close, and proceeded to rub his cheek against mine. That got a big laugh from the entourage. Leaning back but still holding my shoulders, he stared at me for what seemed like forever. Finally, he smiled.

"Go check the mirror," he said. "You'll see that it doesn't come off."

My face turned shades of red I can't even imagine. Probably candy-apple.

Sammy's Sunday brunches were legendary, although sometimes a little odd. Once when I entered his house, Alma directed me to Sammy and his wife's bedroom. When I opened the door, there they were, the two of them, still in bed and totally naked, reading Ian Fleming "James Bond" books. They nodded at me as if this was something totally normal.

The brunches were prepared by Alma and they were always excellent. She also made the best fried chicken in the world. But once, Alma was not the one to greet me when I came to the house. That was odd. And then during the brunch, we ran out of scrambled eggs; normally, this never happened.

"Where's Alma?" I asked. "Is she on vacation?"

Sammy looked around at the rest of us and sheepishly grinned.

"Only in America," he muttered. "Alma quit. She up and left me and went down to Long Beach." He paused for a second. "And . . . she bought a hotel . . ."

That caught everyone at the table by surprise. Sammy continued.

". . . so, if we want her eggs, I guess we'll have to go down to Long Beach." He picked at a piece of fruit on his plate, then looked back at us. "I guess I was paying her too much."

You think?!

I made it to Las Vegas almost every time Sammy was performing. I took regular steam baths there with the guys: Frank, Dean, and Sammy, but also Pat Henry, Joey Bishop, and Peter Lawford. It's funny: the last time I saw Peter Lawford, he was at the Playboy Mansion in L.A. I happened to walk into the library, and there he was sitting at Hef's desk, gray hair down to his shoulders, talking to Johnny Crawford, the actor who played Chuck Connors' son on *The Rifleman*. I didn't want to interrupt, so I left the room. It was strange but I never saw Peter again, although I still run into Johnny at the Mansion from time to time.

In 1990 at the age of sixty-four, Sammy passed away. He was much too young. Maybe the years of high living and the drugs had taken their toll; I don't know. I had attended a lot of Davis family funerals and now here was another one. I virtually buried Sammy's entire family.

It was a sad spring day when they laid Sammy to rest. In his biography, there's a picture of me with John Russell and him from our time together on *Lawman*. I'm proud that Sammy thought so much of me to include that picture in his book. At the time, I thought, maybe I can return the favor some day.

This book is that day.

It's sad that all the Rat Pack . . . uh, I mean "Summit" men are gone, but the legacies they left behind will be remembered for years. I have a final story to tell about the boys, one that I always look back upon fondly.

I was on a publicity trip to Seattle when I got a call from Sammy. "The Boss wants you to join us in Chicago," he said. "We're doing a big show for the Chicago Urban League. Dean, me, . . . everybody's here."

"Count me in, " I replied.

"Do you have any of your cowboy stuff with you?"

"Sure," I said, "I'm doing a *Lawman* publicity gig here. I've got my gun, holster, and hat . . . everything but my horse. Why do you ask?"

"Frank wants you to bring it all. We'll send a plane to pick you up. Can you leave right away?"

A plane to pick me up?! Aren't I Mr. Bigshot?!

"Peter, I said can you leave right away?" he reiterated.

"Are you kidding?!" I replied. "Hell yes!"

This thing was really going to be big. The Chicago Urban League was putting on a Jazz Festival; their other performers included Dizzy Gillespie, "Cannonball" Adderly, Maynard Ferguson and his band, and comic Nipsy Russell.

Sammy arranged everything for me, and so on August 27, 1960, within a few hours of talking with him, I was luxuriating in a private jet on my way to Chicago. On the tarmac, a limousine picked me up and whisked me away. Sammy's shadow, Murphy Bennett, was in the limo. On the way, he filled me in. The Chicago Urban League benefit was a huge event being held in Comiskey Park, home of the Chicago White Sox professional baseball team. The money raised was earmarked for local charities.

So there I sat, a young actor very excited about the prospects of the evening. Now, although I knew Sammy and Dean reasonably well, at that time I had only met Frank a few times, so my excitement was tempered with a small tinge of fear. Murphy led me down into the innards of the park, finally reaching the players' locker room. All the guys were there: Sammy, Frank, Dean, Edd

"Kookie" Byrnes, and a host of others. They had a bar set up and were all heavily in their cups. It was at that moment that it finally dawned on me:

I should be nervous! I mean, what the hell am I going to do for 40,000 people?

I cornered Sammy and desperately asked, "What am I going to do? I'm sure not going to sing and I don't think a fast-draw demonstration will translate for the thousands of people here."

Sammy thought a moment, screwing up his face the way only he could. Then, an idea popped into his head. He thought it was brilliant.

"Just wing it."

I stared at him in disbelief.

"That's what we do," he added.

"But I'm not you guys!" I exclaimed. "I work from a script!"

Fortunately, Frank noticed my panic and came over to calm me down. His words definitely helped.

"Why don't you just introduce Sammy?" he asked. He was trying to hide it, but I sensed he was a bit exasperated. "You can handle that, can't you, kid?"

I nodded appreciatively, in my mind saying, *Yes, that sounds like something I can handle.*

So, I was introduced shortly thereafter and went out on stage to introduce Sammy. The place was packed and the audience gave me a tremendous welcome complete with thunderous applause. They must have all been *Lawman* fans.

I began telling stories, starting with how I happened to be there that night, that when Frank Sinatra asks you to come, YOU COME! That got a nice laugh.

As I continued, it seemed as if, somehow, whatever I said came out funny. I was getting more laughs . . . big laughs! I noticed off-stage an anxious Sammy waiting and pacing, but I was having such a great time out there that I was in no hurry to give up the spot-

On stage with "The Rat Pack"; Edd Byrnes, Peter Lawford, Sammy Davis Jr. and Frank Sinatra.

light. I was definitely enjoying this.

After a few minutes more of what I thought was witty banter, I looked again. A more upset Sammy was now giving me the "throat-slashing" gesture, roughly meaning "shut your blithering mouth and get the hell off the stage!" So I did.

"Ladies and gentlemen," I said into the microphone. My voice boomed all over the stadium. "Here is my very good pal, Mr. Sammy Davis Jr."

Sammy came out, glaring at me out of his one good eye. We locked stares for a moment; as usual, he broke up first. I loved every minute of it.

Later in the show, they called me back onto the stage to sing with them. Think of it! Me, singing with the Rat Pack! I still have a picture from that night of me with the guys.

The next morning at the hotel, while still enjoying the high from the previous evening's activities, I was packing my stuff when for the life of me I couldn't find my gun. It was the Colt 45 I wore on *Lawman*. Everybody I checked with said they had no idea what happened to it: Sammy, Frank, the room maid. Nobody had seen it. I began to panic.

I was scheduled to shoot an episode of *Lawman* on Monday, so with trepidation in my voice, I called the studio and got a hold of our prop guy. I felt a little better when he told me he had a "double gun," an exact replica of mine, and would bring it to the set, but I was still upset about the missing pistol.

I continued searching, doing everything possible to find my gun. I mean, it had been specially made to fit my hand, weighted just right, so I just hated the idea of losing it.

Finally, with all avenues of search exhausted, I left despondently for the airport. Frank and Sammy had both already departed. I was one downhearted cowboy on the flight back to L.A.

On Monday morning, I went to my dressing room as usual. And lo and behold, there on the chair by my makeup mirror was ... MY GUN! I breathed a huge sigh of relief.

It was sitting there pretty as you please, almost as if a beneficent light was shining down upon it. There was an elegant envelope sitting nearby with my name handwritten in calligraphy on it.

I clutched the gun to my heart with one hand, afraid to let it go, and ripped open the envelope with the other. I unfolded the card and held it up to the light. On it was just one sentence:

Sammy put me up to this.

It was signed by Frank Sinatra.

"Why, I've got to tell you,
I am a huge fan of Lawman."
— Hugh Hefner

Chapter 10
Mr. Hugh Hefner

During my fifty-five-plus years in show business, I've met many celebrities, ranging from the raving divas with outsized egos all the way down to the salt-of-the-earth, self-effacing Everyman who just happens to have that special talent for entertaining people. But a chance meeting in 1959 with perhaps the most interesting, and most misunderstood, man occurred while I was doing a promotional tour for a Warner Brothers film. The movie was *The Young Philadelphians*; the man was Hugh Hefner. And now some fifty-three years later, I still consider him to be one of my best friends.

Strangely enough, I wasn't even in the movie I was promoting. Since it was a Warner Brothers picture, and since I was under a Warner Brothers contract, the studio figured they'd put me to work going around the country promoting *The Young Philadelphians*. It sounds weird now, but that was common practice back in those days.

So there I was in Chicago at the Ambassador East Hotel to do a radio interview with Irv Kupcinet. Irv was a longtime newspaper columnist for the *Chicago Sun-Times* and was also a big broadcast personality. He had his own radio show where he staged interviews in a huge circular booth in the dining room of the Ambassador East Hotel.

When I arrived that fateful day, I was led to Irv's booth where he was sitting with a thin-faced man who was smoking a pipe. The pipe smoke seemed to curl up around him, giving his face a hazy, almost mystic aura. The pipe-smoker looked up and nodded. Then it hit me:

I know this man!

My mind raced for a second, trying to match a name with the face. It soon dawned on me: This was Mr. Playboy himself, Hugh Hefner.

Now, any young man growing up in the fifties was readily aware of who Hugh Hefner was. I'm sure all of us guys at one time or another had swiped copies of our dad's *Playboy* magazines, then smuggled them into our bedrooms and slyly stashed them beneath our mattresses, confident there was no way that Mom would be able to find our buried cache of pulp gold in such a clever hiding place, at least not before such a time as we could be alone with the girls of *Playboy*. And now there I was, face to face with the great man, the idol of half the country's population. I stood there, awestruck, not knowing if I should speak to him and, if so, what I should say.

Irv broke the ice by introducing the two of us.

"Peter Brown," Hef said as we shook hands.

I continued to stand there transfixed. He looked directly at me and smiled.

"Yes . . . uh, yes, I am," I managed to stammer out. "I'm a big fan of *Playboy* magazine."

"Why, I've got to tell you, I am a big — no, make that "huge" fan of *Lawman*. You are very good."

"You're a fan of mine?!" I think my voice squeaked. "That is so nice of you to say." I quickly grew more comfortable, more confident. "And as a man who adores beautiful women," I offered, "just let me say for every man out there in the country, thank you for all that you've done for us."

"So what are you going to talk about with Irv?" he asked.

"Oh, the interview is mainly going to be about a movie in which I don't appear."

Hef laughed. "I may have to stay and hear about this movie in which you don't appear."

After the interview, Hef and I sat and talked for quite a while. There was so much I wanted to ask him, but he was so unpretentious that he kept bringing the conversation back to me. Finally as he got up to go, he turned back, took a big drag on his pipe, and then somehow blew a smoke ring that I imagined was in the shape of the *Playboy* rabbit-head logo.

"Come on over to the Mansion tonight," he said. "There's dinner and a movie in it for you . . . and a lot of interesting men and women . . . especially the women."

"I'll be there, Mr. Hefner," I said eagerly.

"I'm looking forward to your visit. And please. Call me 'Hef.' All my friends call me Hef."

"Well, thank you, Hef."

And that's how our friendship of a half-century's duration began. Hef's mansions have become home-away-from-homes for me.

I remember that first night I went to the Playboy Mansion in Chicago. I had taken a cab, not knowing what to expect regarding parking, drinking, and accommodations. I told the driver the address.

"Ohhh," he beamed, "you're going to the Playboy Mansion. I guess I don't have to tell you to enjoy yourself."

When we arrived, I went to the massive entryway and rang the bell. A distinguished older gentleman opened the door.

"Good evening, Mr. Brown, " he said, it sounding more like an announcement than a greeting. "Hef has been expecting you. He's waiting down in the bar. Just follow this hallway past the pool. You'll come to a circular staircase and a fireman's pole. They both lead down to the bar. Just pick the one you like."

Of course me being me, I had to take the pole. It was exactly my style. As I passed the pool, I spotted some girls swimming, some with tiny swimsuits on, some with even less. I started grinning.

I'm going to like this place! I thought to myself.

There was a guest book on a table downstairs. A beautiful (that term is going to become redundant in this chapter) young woman dressed in a bunny outfit greeted me.

"Hi! My name is Joannie. If you need anything at all tonight, just let me know. And be sure to sign Hef's guest book before you leave. Hef likes to keep a record of all his guests."

I signed in with all my info. Sure enough, on my return to L.A., I found a note from Hef waiting inviting me to the Playboy Mansion West. Now so many years later, I am still being invited every Sunday night to the Mansion for dinner and a movie. I am one lucky guy.

Hef is ten years older than me, but going back to the day we met, I've always felt like his contemporary. He has a knack for making you feel like the most important person in the world. All these years later, I've come to see him as probably the kindest and most astute person I've ever met. He is certainly the most gracious man I know.

In essence, Hef is a very simple man; it's the way he treats people that makes him so different from most ultra-rich, big-shot executives. Whenever I would go to the West Coast Mansion, there he'd be holding court at the head of the dining room table with people milling about everywhere. I would arrive and immediately seek him out in the midst of the hubbub in order to pay my respects. With all the people surrounding him, I never expected anything more than a cursory "Hello" from him. But the great thing about

With KK and Hef.

Hef is, he invariably grabs your hand and makes you feel welcome. And when we talk, there's none of that "looking over your shoulder" business to see if somebody better has just come in. I unfailingly have his full attention for as long as we talk. And it wasn't just me; that's how he is with everyone. He's a true gentleman and a friend to all.

The West Coast Playboy Mansion is in Holmby Hills, California, but when you get there, you think you're in heaven, Playboy heaven. There's an outside bar near the pool. All the food and drinks are provided by Hef. Back then, as long as Hef was there, his friends were always welcome. The front door was never locked. And for a young actor, at least during those times when I was unmarried, it was the ultimate setting for meeting women. It didn't hurt that these were the most beautiful women in the world. On more than one occasion, I had the good fortune of having a *Play-*

boy Bunny or Playmate accompany me home.

In addition to the Mansion, Hef owns another house just down the street. It's used as a place to stay for out-of-town Bunnies and potential playmates. He also bought the house next door for his ex-wife Kimberley Conrad and their two young sons, Marston and Cooper, to live. Hef and Kimberley had been married in July of 1989, but they separated in 1998. They divorced in 2009 when Cooper, the younger of their sons, reached eighteen-years of age.

Hef loves having people around, especially at holiday time. Christmas is big at his household; we regularly send him a card at Christmas and try to have a gift for him on his birthday. People will ask me, "What do you give a man who has everything?" And I have to agree. Remember, this is Hugh Hefner; he is not an easy man to shop for. One year, we gave him homemade rum balls; my wife KK fashioned some very fancy truffles with different flavors and decor. Hef really loved those. And he's a big movie fan, so on another birthday, we gave him a Turner Classic Movie trivia game along with a boxed DVD-set of my *Laredo* television series. Hef genuinely appreciates simple yet well-thought out gifts.

Easter is an even bigger holiday at the Mansion. Beyond the usual assortment of Easter ducks, chicks, and bunnies, real bunnies, Hef has a world-class petting zoo for the kids that includes a camel, an alligator, turtles, a baby fox, a kangaroo, and more. It's perfect for entertaining the little ones. He loves when the kids, children of friends and former playmates, are there. He caters to them completely. There's invariably an enormous Easter egg hunt . . . make that "hunts." To ensure that every child finds at least one egg, he has multiple Easter egg hunts broken down by age. And there are big prizes for the kids. I still go, even though my kids are way past that age, just to be there. That event inevitably brings a smile to my face.

A more common event, happening almost weekly, are Hef's movie nights. He loves to entertain by screening favorite movies right there at the Mansion. Hef is a bona fide connoisseur of cinema. He has amassed a most unbelievable film library at the Mansion. He loves hosting movie parties with screenings most Friday, Saturday, and Sunday nights. A sign on the bar always lets you know what movie will be running that night and at what time, usually 6:30 p.m. In his screening room, about fifty people can be accommodated. His movie nights are so popular that the competition for seats can be quite fierce at times. During the week of April 9th, which happens to be Hef's birthday, he always shows *Casablanca*, his all-time favorite film. The really fun part of *Casablanca* night is that while we're watching Humphrey Bogart, Ingrid Bergman, Peter Lorre, and Paul Henreid, the nearby dining room is being converted into the Moroccan "Rick's Café" right out of the movie. On those nights, we celebrate Hef's birthday wearing white jackets like Bogey as the champagne flows and the caviar is enjoyed.

Movies have always been Hef's favorite hobby. One of the things he absolutely loves to do is organize a group trip to the movies. Usually he'll take a bunch of us to 842 South Broadway in downtown L.A. to the old Orpheum Theater. The Orpheum is a wonderful place. Opened in 1926 as a vaudeville venue, the Orpheum has hosted some of the most revered names spanning the history of show business: burlesque queen Sally Rand, the young Francis Gumm (later known as "Judy Garland"), Jack Benny, Lena Horne, and Duke Ellington. During my years on television, the theater got more into rock and roll, featuring such music industry greats as Stevie Wonder, Aretha Franklin, and Little Richard. In addition to classic movies, they still welcome live performances and special events to their mythical stage.

On Orpheum night, Hef will hire a bus and take fifty of us out on the town. To preserve the atmosphere he wants for his friends, he reserves the entire theater. Once seated, we watch whichever movie Hef has selected for the evening. It doesn't matter what he chooses. Hef's an aficionado of all well-made films; he never disappoints.

After all these years, I still get invites to Hef's parties. For a long time, there was a core group of us who inevitably showed up: Cornell Wilde, bandleader Ray Anthony, Robert Culp, and Mel Torme, just to name a few. We could arrive at any time, all of us with standing invitations from Hef. And Hef was not just locked into the entertainment industry; he was well connected everywhere. The Mansion was an incredible place to meet the widest assortment of interesting people, shakers and movers from all walks of life.

On July 20, 1969, I was in a small town in Israel making a movie. There was only one television set in the village. Luckily, it was located in the lobby of our little hotel. We all gathered together late that night to watch Neil Armstrong and Buzz Aldrin become the first men to walk on the moon.

Now, skip ahead a few years. I'm at the Mansion, enjoying the crowd, the music, just the atmosphere in general. A pleasant looking couple approaches me and introduce themselves. To my amazement, it's the same moon-walking astronaut I, and the rest of the world, had watched so many years ago. Buzz Aldrin and his lovely wife Lois couldn't have been nicer. We hit it off right away and now are always glad to see each other when we're both at the Mansion. The funny thing is, in all those years of conversations, we've never talked about his experiences on the moon. It's all pretty much just guy stuff, and that's the way we both like it.

Away from the Mansion in the world of business, Hef's magazine and my show-business careers crossed paths only once. Once was apparently more than enough. Our joint venture received a ton of attention, some good, some not so much. As with anything Hef got involved in, it produced much commentary on both sides of the issue.

In the fall of 1972, Playboy Enterprises had purchased the U.S. rights to a French magazine titled *Lui* and had changed the title to *Oui*. In trying to spice up an already spicy publication, Hef had asked me to do a magazine layout for him. Now, he knew that I had previously rejected offers, very lucrative offers I might add, to do nude pictures for the magazines *Playgirl* and *Viva*.

Not that I was ashamed of my body, but those guys wanted to show just a bit too much. But with Hef, I knew it would be different. He was a man I could trust. He promised me his shoot would be tastefully done; he even gave me full editorial approval over which pictures would be used. Hef had been so good to me for so long that I felt if he wanted me to do it, then I wanted to do it. The fact that I was already very popular as Dr. Greg Peters on the daytime soap opera *Days of Our Lives* didn't hurt. I had a lot of positives going for me in this shoot. We sealed the deal with a handshake, which is how I like to do business. In fact, the name of my current production company reflects just that: "Handshake Films."

Oui was somewhat similar to *Playboy* with its nude photos of beautiful people, both men and women, as well as centerfolds, interviews and articles, and cartoons. The tone of the magazine was changed just enough to keep it consistent with Hef's philosophies about sex which had always appealed to *Playboy's* more mature and sophisticated readers. *Oui's* aim, while staying true to Hef's beliefs, was to reach a younger audience. Photo layouts like mine were an avenue to reach that goal. In the end though, Hef figured out that *Oui* was taking too many readers away from *Playboy*, the parent publication, so in June of 1981, Playboy Enterprises pulled the plug on its new magazine and sold it to a New York publishing house.

Back to my shoot. In November of 1974, my photo session commenced. It was done on a very isolated and deserted beach way down at the end of Cabo San Lucas, Mexico. It was remote, in fact so remote that you could get to it only by boat. Regrettably, the remoteness of the shoot failed to assuage my lovely young co-star. When it came time for the shoot to start, she developed an acute case of "stage fright"; I'm sure she had second thoughts about what her parents might think of her appearing nude before the camera. *Playboy* had to send her home. Fortunately, her replacement had no such qualms, and we got started just a bit behind schedule.

The shoot was very professionally done. Hef rented a house there for me. The well-known photographer Arnie Freytag was assigned to take the pictures. The producer had a definite theme for the two of us doing the shoot, much more romantic and playful than just posed pictures of naked bodies. They really seemed to know what they were doing. I was elated to be able to take part in the shoot in the sun and fun with a beautiful young lady in the most scenic of locations.

The photo shoot got off to a very painful start. On the first day, I was in the kitchen of the rented house. I had just taken one of those old ice-cube trays out of the freezer and had dumped the ice into the sink. Unfortunately for me, when I reached down to grab one of the loose cubes, a scorpion, always preferring moist areas, resented my intrusion into his habitat and stung my hand. Now that was painful. I grabbed a knife and slashed at the bite spot on my hand, then tried to suck out the poison.

They immediately called for a doctor, but as isolated as we were, there was no clinic nearby. It took what seemed like forever for medical assistance to arrive. When the local doctor arrived, I was able to speak just enough Spanish to let him know what happened. He took one look at my surgical technique and told me, thankfully, that I had done the right thing.

The pictures turned out great, just me and my beautiful friend frolicking nude on the beach. It all felt very innocent, reminiscent of the previous decade's free love and flower power images. Still, the pictures were published in an adult magazine. No matter what the tenor of the shoot, controversy was bound to follow.

And follow it did. At the time, the *Days of Our Lives* bigwigs weren't sure what to make of my *Playboy* exposure. Although it had been my right, I hadn't personally screened all the photographs. I simply relied on Hef's expertise and judgment. The few questionable photos that were taken were brought to me by Hef for my thumbs-up or thumbs down. I really appreciated his concern for my feelings. One somewhat cropped picture caused a lot of anxiety in the world of daytime drama. It was highlighted that spring by an interview I did with the soap magazine *Afternoon TV Stars*. It led with the following headline: "Those Controversial Nude Photos of Peter Brown — Why He Did It!"

Fortunately, soaps being soaps, the bottom line of this supposedly sordid little affair was how did it affect the ratings. And judging by the huge increase of fan letters I received and the corresponding ratings boost, the producers seemed relieved, if not happy, about my spread in *Oui*.

I was happy to have been able to work with Hef. He's a man I've always greatly respected. To this day, I am proud to call him my friend.

"What the hell was I thinking?"
— The phrase I often muttered after introducing
Ann-Margret to Roger Smith, her future husband

Chapter 11

Redheads, Bullfights & Other Friends

One of the greatest things about a career in the entertainment industry, as you might guess, is the incredible people you meet on your journey through the show business life. Oh sure, the money's great, the fame is wonderful, the women are . . . are . . . what was I talking about?

Oh yeah, the people.

Who am I kidding? My life was all so great and exciting, almost every day. But the people, they're what I'll remember best from my nearly seventy years in the business. So in this chapter, I'm going to talk about some of the special people that meant so much to me, whether it was just for a day or for a lifetime. And since my partiality must be showing throughout this tome, I'm going to bookend this segment with a pair of redheads. Let's start with one of my favorite entertainers of all time: Ann-Margret.

This gorgeous lady can still do it all: sing, dance, and act. She has had a career for the ages: two each Oscar and Grammy nominations; five Golden Globe wins; and six Emmy nominations with one win. She appeared in the the film *Bye Bye Birdie* and starred in *Viva Las Vegas* with Elvis Presley. She's also somehow found the time to make fourteen albums in her illustrious career. As I said, she's done it all. And I like to think I had a small, oh-so small part in it all, at least at the beginning.

Ann's big break was getting hooked up with Pierre Cossette as her personal manager. He was very well connected in the industry. She signed with him; I had nothing to do with her getting him as a rep. I did, however, try to help get her a music contract by introducing her around at Warner Brothers. I spoke to Carl Engeman, the head of Warners' music department. He agreed to give her a listen, so I set up an appointment with her and Carl. After their get-together, there was no doubt that he liked what he heard. He liked Ann so much, in fact, that he immediately went to the head of the company, Jack Warner, to offer him this jewel. Going to see Jack, unfortunately, was a mistake.

"What are we going to do with another pretty girl singer?" Jack responded. "We already have Connie Stevens under contract."

So, amazingly, Warner Brothers passed on her. And that's how Jack Warner screwed up the signing of the now legendary Ann-Margret.

But it would take more than Jack Warner's shortsightedness to derail this effervescent girl's career. Soon after, Pierre got Ann the opportunity to sing an Oscar nominated song on the 1962 Academy Awards show. That night she belted out "Bachelor in Paradise" and her career was launched.

While our social lives intersected quite often in the sixties, we only worked together once, that being in 1964 on the infamous *Kitten with a Whip* movie shot on the back lot of Paramount at night. By then, there was no denying it to myself: I was flat out in love with her. I have no idea how things progressed to us ending up more as friends than as boyfriend-girlfriend. In an unusual twist, it was a case where friendship overcame romance. But Ann was such a wonderful person, I'd take whatever I could get.

I'll have to admit that I did recently sneak a peak at Ann's biography to, uh . . . to just get her view on our relationship . . . yeah, that's what I did. I found out one of the things she always remembered and admired about me was how wonderful I was to my fans.

Really?! Hmmm . . . I guess I'll have to take it.

Oh, I have to admit she's probably right on that point. I was very conscious of "Peter Brown nation." I always obliged my fans, unless that is, they were rude; I would not tolerate that. I never refused an autograph request except if it was spurred on by some sort of mania. Early in my career, a bunch of girls camped out by my hotel suite. How they got in there and found my room I'll never know. I do know that as soon as I got off the elevator, they went nuts. It was all I could do to keep from being sacked at the five-yard line. Once I did get them calmed down, not an easy task I must say, I signed all their autograph books.

That was the way I did it; I never let things go too far. I've had young women pull out their breasts and asked me to sign them. And as tempting as it was, I never did it. It just didn't seem right, and besides, it would just be opening the door for the next girl to want something more, whatever that might be. I never minded signing autographs; I even signed two just the other day. It's when they stop asking for your autograph that it's time to start worrying.

Back to Ann-Margret. My marriage to Diane had recently ended, freeing me up to get out there and start meeting women again. I first spotted Ann in Newport Beach where she was doing a club date with "The Scott Smith Trio"; it was a summer job for her. I noticed her right away; she's still such a different girl the moment she comes out on stage. I was immediately infatuated with this lovely young lady. After seeing several of her shows, I worked up the nerve to introduce myself. Just like that, I had a date.

Over the course of the summer, we saw each other many times. I even took her to several Hollywood parties and premieres. That was her first introduction to the glitter and hoopla of "Hollywood." I also found out she had never been to Disneyland, so I arranged to take her, her parents, and one of her good friends to the Magic

Kingdom. Nothing like a little "Mickey Mouse" to cement a relationship.

I did what I could for her young career, setting up appointments for and introducing her to any influential people I thought might help. I had seen how talented she was; I just wanted to get her the exposure she needed. I even got her an apartment at my complex on Sunset Boulevard, the same place where my experience with my gay landlord almost cost him his life (To refresh your memory, see chapter two).

I was continuing on my merry way helping to mold her young career when I went what turned out to be one step too far: I misguidedly introduced her to Roger Smith. My "buddy" later became her husband in one of the most successful marriages in Hollywood. Boy, talk about shooting yourself in the foot.

It all began on January 17, 1961, when I called Ann. We had dated a few times, but I was still looking for any excuse to see her. After all, she was Ann-Margret! I was traveling to Green Bay, Wisconsin, to appear on a telethon and had a brief stopover in Chicago. I asked her to come to O'Hare Airport, hang out with me, and then, before my plane took off, join me for an early breakfast. "Early" turned out to be 5 a.m.

Ann arrived bright and early the next morning accompanied by her parents whom I also adored. She looked fantastic. I, too, was accompanied by someone, my pal Roger Smith who for three years had been appearing on the hit TV show *77 Sunset Strip*. He was also scheduled to appear on the telethon. Ann, however, apparently didn't watch much TV, so she had no idea who Roger was. I should have left it at that.

I introduced the two of them, then they had a brief conversation. It went something like this:

"So, you're trying to be an actress?"

"Yes."

"How's it going?"

"I was just tested at Twentieth Century Fox."

"Good luck. Maybe we'll see each other sometime in L.A."

"Sure."

And that was about it. Innocent enough. Roger later said to me, referring to Ann, "Poor thing. That sweet, innocent baby will be devoured by the wolves out in Hollywood." His perceived lack of confidence in her was somehow reassuring to me.

The five of us had breakfast, then Ann kissed me goodbye and told Roger that it had been very nice to meet him. She had been pleasant enough and was polite to him, but I could tell there were no sparks flying. I'm very perceptive at reading situations like that.

Apparently, not perceptive enough. Six years later, they got married.

O.K., no more kidding around. Roger is such a nice guy that I couldn't really be mad at him for breaking the "bro" code. Besides, I was never really the jealous type. I don't feel one person can ever "own" another; that type of control just doesn't work. In the end, we all became good friends.

I still helped her out as much as I could, her being new to southern California and all. Later when I lived in Benedict Canyon on Hutton Drive in Beverly Hills, I found a house nearby for Ann just up the hill from me. It's funny when I think back to the time Ann wanted a deck built. Still competing with each other, Roger and I each wanted to build it. Unfortunately for me, when it came to construction, where he was an excellent carpenter, I, on the other hand, was an excellent actor. He built it, they dated, and soon I was out of the picture. But I love those two and how happy they are together. And whenever I see them, I close my eyes and fondly think back a few years. And all I can say about introducing these two wonderful people is:

"WHAT THE HELL WAS I THINKING?!"

Besides actually working with so many greats in the business, I had other celebrity interactions in some of the strangest places. I once needed a table for my dining room, so I checked around and found just what I was looking for. Turns out it was owned by Dick Martin of the famous comedy team, "Rowan and Martin." A few years later, they would go on to dominate the nation's viewing habits with their landmark TV show, *Rowan and Martin's Laugh-In.* Dick and Dan actually owned a house together. Funny as it may seem, they were having a tag sale, so that's where I went with all the other weekend scavengers to buy my table. Actually, I just called them up and bought it.

I was acquainted with other people in other ways. Prior to the elections sometime in the mid-sixties, I got politically involved with, of all people, Marlon Brando. He had assembled a group of his pals, including Dennis Hopper, to go down south to Selma, Alabama, to help in a march for equal rights. Somehow, I became part of that scene, although I must admit that was more politics than I had ever gotten involved with before or after.

Then there was the time I was doing a TV guest shot on *The Streets of San Francisco* with Karl Malden and Michael Douglas. While on location, I heard mention that the great Ella Fitzgerald was singing at a local saloon. I had briefly met her once before through Sammy, so I made my way downtown and grabbed a seat for her show. When she finished, she came down off the stage and took a seat nearby with friends as another performer went on.

Come to think of it, that really had to be tough: Following Ella Fitzgerald!

Anyway, I wanted to pay my respects, so I walked over to her table, extended my hand, re-introduced myself while telling her how much I had enjoyed her singing. She was very nice and thanked me profusely. I was just so excited to be able to talk to her. But here's the funny thing: as I left her table, I heard her say to her friends, "See?! I told you I knew Peter Brown."

See?! I told you I knew Peter Brown.

Sorry for the repetition. I just like the thought of her saying that.

That statement came as a complete surprise to me. The great Ella Fitzgerald had just paid me one of the nicest compliments I've ever received. Ah, show business.

I was able to meet another legendary singer, this time though with slightly different results. I had gone to the Hollywood Bowl with my old army buddy, Dick Deneut, to hear Harry Belafonte sing. Dick was a writer and a photographer for Globe Photos, a company which had some connections with Belafonte's people, so after an absolutely wonderful performance, Dick was able to get me backstage to meet Harry. That was pretty exciting stuff.

While we were talking with the great singer, I noticed he had a giant rack full of the most beautiful shirts. I was entranced by their color and variety.

"Where did you ever get such beautiful shirts?" I exclaimed as I massaged their material between my thumb and forefinger. I really wanted to know, figuring I had to pick some up for myself.

"Well," he said slowly, giving me what I thought seemed like a suspicious eye, "I have them made in the east . . . and I sell them in the west."

We shared an uncomfortable moment. Then it hit me:

Harry Belafonte thinks I'm asking for a freebie, a handout. He's saying without saying that if I want one, I'm going to have to pay for it!

I quickly changed the subject. I've never been one to be accused of being cheap, and I certainly didn't want to start then with "The Tally Man." And for the record, I never did get any of his shirts.

One of the biggest surprises of my life occurred on a night I went to the Playboy Mansion in Chicago for another of Hef's spectacular parties. I hopped out of my cab, strode to the front door, and rang the bell. After a moment or two, the giant door swung open. My mouth dropped as I stared in total surprise. That evening I was being greeted not by one of Hef's usual employees but by somebody a little bit overqualified for the position:

It was the Reverend Jessie Jackson.

This incongruous juxtaposition of a great man of the cloth at the home of a great man of the skin left me speechless. Jessie smiled once the reason for my consternation dawned on him.

"In answer you your unasked question," he said, "No, I don't work here. I was just walking by when I heard the bell."

We stared at each other for a moment, then everything came back into focus. We both cracked up laughing. And then I entered, somewhat awkwardly, a Playboy party with the conscience of the nation. Weird!

I also had quite a crew of non-celebrity friends. One of my favorite guys was Robert Raymond from Brisbane, Australia. Like most Aussies I've known, Robert was always looking for a good time.

He was once visiting me at my place on the ocean which was located on "the Strand" in Manhattan Beach. We were sitting on the patio, just a few feet from the ocean, having a few libations when a stunningly gorgeous young woman walked by. Never one to miss an opportunity, Robert immediately made his presence known.

"Here's to you, luv!" he called out as he raised his wine glass in a toast to her beauty. "Can I buy you a drink?!"

I'm sure she had heard that line hundreds of times before. Oh so briefly, she glanced back over her shoulder, checked us out, and then continued on her beach walk. Her distant expression never changed. That setback, however, was not near enough to discourage my friend from down under.

"Well, then . . . can I buy you a car?!"

That was the line that struck pay dirt. Our beautiful girl slammed on the brakes, did a perfect about-face, and then came briskly striding back toward us. By the time she reached the patio, Robert had already poured her a big glass of wine. He then proceeded to charm her the socks off her . . . so to speak. They spent the rest of the afternoon together . . . and most of the evening. Ah, the life of living at the beach.

I have many other stories about my sightings of Hollywood personalities, famous and otherwise, but you've probably got clothes in the dryer, so as promised, I'll finish up with my other celebrity-redhead story. This one involves Stephanie Powers and the national sport of Mexico.

Let me set the stage. During the *Lawman* years, I had started going down to Tijuana for some weekend getaways. On a totally random happenstance, I went into a store, the Casa de Cambio, to exchange dollars for pesos. Simple enough. It turned out the Casa de Cambio was a place where you could buy authentic bullfighting equipment from Spain: clothing, capotes (cloaks), sombreros, all the real stuff. As is my style, I got to talking to the owner of the shop, Paco Ros Oviedo, and before you knew it, I had a new friend. He introduced me to his wife, Betty, and daughter Marina. They were all lovely people.

Now skip ahead a few years. I was dating the gorgeous redhead Stephanie Powers at the time; we weren't going together exclusively although we did end up seeing each other for a year or two. Stephanie and I were really more friends than boyfriend-girlfriend. We always stayed on good terms with each other. Still, I just adored her; I'm so glad we remained friends.

Anyway, I asked her to come along with me on one of my regular trips to Tijuana. Paco had invited us to stay with him and his family. Old school rules prevailed at the Oviedo household; since Stephanie and I weren't married, he wouldn't allow us to share a bedroom. That was fine with me . . . well, maybe not "fine," but when in Rome . . .

On his property, Paco had a second, smaller house that he rented out to a jai alai player named Alberto Doggins. Just the nicest guy, Alberto invited Steph and me to come watch him play.

I describe the sport of jai alai like this: it's like a giant racquetball court with one side open to the audience. Instead of racquets, players have giant scoops (called "cestas") which they use to catch and fling against the wall. It's called the fastest ball game in the world with slung throws approaching 185 miles an hour. Spectators bet on the participants just like betting on the horses at any racing track in the States.

Trying to be supportive, we bet on Alberto to win . . . and much to our surprise and delight, he did! In fact, he won every game he played that night. It finally dawned on us that Alberto must have told all his jai alai buddies that two big-time Hollywood actors were his guests at the fronton (arena) that day. Wanting to make sure he looked good, they were subtly, if you can play jai alai "subtly," letting him win. We didn't feel right about that, so we quit betting on him. It was a little embarrassing, although no one said anything. Everybody at the fronton acted as if it was business as usual.

While we were there, I wanted to impress Stephanie with my vast knowledge of the Spanish language. I puffed up as I went to the window where they rented seat cushions.

"Senor," I said confidently, "dos cajones por favor."

"Que?" he replied.

"Dos cajones por favor!" I reiterated impatiently. I got the strangest look from the little man behind the counter.

"No tienes nada, senor?" he snorted derisively.

A guy back in line stepped forward and tapped me on the shoulder.

"Hey mister, you just asked him for two 'balls,' not 'seat cushions.' He's asking you, 'Don't you have any? Don't you have any balls?'"

As you can tell once you stop laughing, I obviously got the

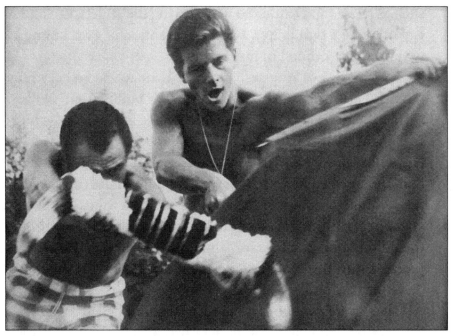

Bullfight practice in Griffith Park.

Spanish word cojine (cushion) mixed up with the Spanish word "cajones" (the aforementioned "balls"). Stephanie tried to hide her laughter, but she didn't do doing a very good job. It took me quite a while to live that one down.

Paco also introduced me to Jaime Bravo, a well-known Mexican matador (bullfighter . . . I'm pretty sure I got that one right). Jaime actually lived in Los Angeles where he was married to the American actress, Ann Robinson. He invited us to come to one of his bullfights when we were in Tijuana again. We did and enjoyed ourselves enough that we came back for another fight and then another. The pageantry was just spectacular.

I think you can see what's coming. Gradually, I felt the urge to give bullfighting a try. It was the artistry and the tradition of the sport that really appealed to me, not its inherent violence toward animals. And you have to remember that this was a different time and culture. Being a cowboy, I had great respect for ranch animals such as horses and cattle. So while loving the athleticism and strategy of being a bullfighter, I had no intention of ever killing a bull . . . and I never did. I'm just saying.

So back in Los Angeles, Jaime took me to the archery range at Griffith Park where I could practice my "bullfighting" skills. The surface there was packed sand which made it a lot like the bull ring in Tijuana. Jaime had a set of horns mounted on wheels to simulate a charging bull. He would run the horns at me for practice. Sometimes when he wasn't there, Stephanie would run the horns at me. Although not quite the same as having a thousand pounds of angry beef rushing at you, it did allow me to practice my timing for the different kinds of passes Jaime had shown me. He also let me practice with the "banderillas," the sharp sticks that the matadors drive into the bull.

There were two capes we used: a large one called a "capote," and the smaller "muleta." The muleta had a "palillo" (wooden pokey stick) that went through a loop in the cape. Jaime, great guy that he was, even made me a bullfighting suit designed for amateurs or students called a "traje corto." It was a thing of beauty. I wish I still had it. Unfortunately, after my fourth divorce, ex-wife Mary sold it at a garage sale. Can you believe that? Maybe Dick Martin bought it.

I actually got to fight a real bull about a half-dozen times. My fights took place in the old bullring in downtown Tijuana. That first time, boy, I've got to tell you, I was nervous. Of course, Jaime, my teacher and friend, was there as well as Stephanie. I fought during the "quite", a pause during regular bullfights which allows students of the sport to do demonstration fights. Of course, the bulls really don't know the difference. These were the bullfights where I participated. (DISCLAIMER: No animals were harmed in the writing of this chapter or during any of my "fights.")

After my last fight, thankfully I was still in one piece. That's really the best any bullfighter can hope for. Knowing that, I decided

Peter the Bullfighter

to hang up my cape and retire my "traje corto." I decided I liked my beef best medium-rare with a baked potato on the side, not having it chase me around an arena with visions of Peter Tartar as its main dish.

All right, I've taken you from one fabulous redhead (Ann-Margret) to another (Stephanie Powers), although neither of them rate as my all-time favorite. That, of course, would be my gorgeous German wife KK (Hi, Honey!)

O.K., let's finish this thing up and then go get a beer. On to Chapter Twelve.

*"A happy family, children, and the ability
to act as well as Sidney Poitier."*
— Just after my first marriage when
asked what my goals were in life

Chapter 12

The Golden Years

On New Years Eve, 2011, my fifty-three-year show-business career arc came full circle:

Lawman returned to the air on cable TV's Western Channel.

Now another generation of young girls will be able to view the exploits of dashing, young Deputy Johnny McKay while affixing his poster to their bedroom walls . . . of course, those young girls will be in their sixties. Ah . . . you take what you can get.

After my soap opera run ended in the early Nineties, I continued to make appearances on both prime time TV shows and in films well into the new millennium. As I recall (and it's getting tougher every day to do so), my last TV gig was a spring 2000 episode of *JAG*. I still get called for small movie parts all the time, but I don't really need to do those. I'm really pretty happy enjoying the good life in Arizona with my lovely bride KK.

I continue to receive residuals from TV and movies, although after this amount of lapsed time, they're usually very small. Sometimes the postage is more than my payment; I actually received one for seven-cents. Right now I have a check on my desk for $5.02. I receive them infrequently; a nice one was in the mail last week for $111. It's unusual, however, if they're more than $20. They're always for movies, never for *Lawman* or *Laredo*; there was no language ever written into those contracts for residuals. But in any case, it's nice to be remembered remuneratively, no matter how small, for my work.

At present, I still have my production company, Handshake Films. My first company, Red Wine International Films (RWIF), pretty much went dormant after we made *Gentle Savage*. I was doing soaps then, so I didn't have a lot of time or opportunity to grow the company. I had hoped to eventually devote all my time to RWIF, but after months turned into years, I could see the handwriting on the wall. And it said, "If it happens, it happens."

A TV production by Handshake Films that I'm currently working on is called *Shootin' the Breeze*, a documentary-like show about the Western legends and their experiences working in Hollywood during the heyday of the cowboy. It includes great old-time actors such as Johnny Crawford, Robert Fuller, Hugh O'Brien, Clint Walker, Cathy Garver, Michael Dante, and Wyatt McCrea among others. It's a wonderful journey into the lives of the Hollywood cowboy of yesteryear. My business partners in this venture are Wyatt McCrea (the grandson of Joel McCrea) and Greg Long.

We actually came up with the idea for the show when a bunch of us had gotten together to shoot the bull after signing autographs at a western show. The stories related were so funny and interesting that before long, we realized we had the seeds of a very fun show. After staring at each other for a moment, we realized we better get these sessions on tape before we're all "gone with the wind."

We got longtime western aficionado Charlie LeSueur to emcee our "talks." It turned out that a normal episode would see six or seven of us on stage telling our stories in front of a studio audience followed by a Q&A with our fans moderated by me.

I really enjoy getting together with the guys and gals I knew from the cowboy shows back in the fifties and sixties. I especially enjoy my good buddy Michael Dante with whom I go back fifty-five years to our life-changing audition at Warner Brothers. Michael definitely has the gift of gab; he hosts a radio show in Palm Springs, California. It's always a trick to have a microphone in front of him and Cathy Garver; when they get going, you get a three-act play. On *Shootin' the Breeze*, if there's a question for Michael, he can take fifteen minutes to answer it. Fortunately, it's always very interesting what he has to say.

Handshake Films has made some nice instructional shorts over the past twenty years: there's the fun one with celebrities fixing their cars; then there's another on motorcycle safety; and of course, there's my personal favorite, *The Penning Tape*, still probably the best instructional video on the subject out there today. We sold a lot of those tapes, some at shows but later many more on our website. We still get the occasional order for one now and then.

We produced the video tape of this horse event at rodeos. In it, I wore multiple hats: narrator, actor, and producer. Casey Tibbs, the World Champion All-Around Cowboy, did a wonderfully nice intro for it. Sadly, he passed away just six days later. We all really miss him. He was a great guy, a "cowboy's cowboy.".

I may be biased but *The Penning Tape* is truly a superior video. But don't just take my word for it. Six-time all-around champion cowboy Larry Mahan, when asked about the tape, was quoted thusly: "I recommend it for the professional as well as the beginner. This tape offers all the knowledge necessary to become a winner in this great sport."

So there.

Now, you're probably asking yourself as well as six-time all-around champion cowboy Larry Mahan, What the hell is a "penning" tape?

Well, I'm going to tell you. It's the fastest growing equine sport today. Basically, "team" penning is when a trio of riders enters an arena, gallops across the starting line, tries to separate three same-numbered cattle away from a herd of thirty, and then attempts to drive them back over the starting line to the opposite end of the arena into a holding pen, doing all this within a two-minute time limit. I know, it sounds impossible. But these guys and gals can do it. For competitions, winners are determined by the fastest time. This video was especially gratifying for me to make since I'm really into team penning. It's a sport that entails genuine cowhand ranch work.

Another event I liked to get involved in is "Cowboy Mounted Shooting (CMS)." It's kind of a celebrity rodeo thing, although the competition is always heavy duty for those celebs who have excellent riding and shooting skills. It was very big at the Festival of the West in Scottsdale, Arizona.

In CMS, there are nine or ten inflated balloons on sticks in the ground throughout the arena. A competitor wears two holsters, each with a gun holding six blanks. Riding his horse at full speed, he needs to get close enough to the balloon to shoot and burst it, the air pressure from the gun being enough to explode the balloon. Midway through the ride, the contestant has to switch guns while at full gallop. It's a time trial to determine the winner, but any missed balloons cause penalty seconds to be added to a rider's final score, which is based on when his final balloon is broken.

In Scottsdale in 2001, I participated in the CMS competition and was barely edged out by good friend Bruce Boxleitner three days in a row. Man, losing to Bruce three days in a row?! I must have been hung over. Either that or the fix was in.

At another competition that same year, the 20th Annual World Championship of Cowboy Action Shooting in Norco, California, I lost again, although this time it wasn't entirely my fault. I shot the first five balloons perfectly, but as I was then rounding a barrel, I went to change guns. In that instant, I had the surprise of a lifetime: my horse, my "borrowed" horse, reared straight up! With my rhythm and balance thrown totally off by this unexpected turn of events, the horse and I were no longer working as one. He went to the left while I, unfortunately, went flying off to the right, landing most unceremoniously on my hip.

It turned out the event people had assigned me a trained "rearing" horse, not quite appropriate for what I was trying to accomplish. They did let me have a re-ride on a different horse. I had really been flying that first round, but now my enthusiasm was a bit diminished after being thrown. I was still able to take third-place in the event, but I know I could have done better had I rode the proper horse the first time.

I still love being involved in celebrity charity sporting events such as tennis, golf, and rodeo, although now in my mid-Seventies, I don't actively participate as much. I think my last golf outing was three years ago, the last tennis event was probably around 2000. I continue to make appearances at collectors' shows, particularly those oriented to the fans of "Westerns." I just got back from doing the "National Harvest Festival" in Branson, Missouri. It was a blast. I appeared on stage with legendary western star Buck Taylor which was just so much fun. Buck is an incredible painter, famous worldwide for his water colors. I have quite a few of his paintings hanging on the walls of my home.

I really enjoy the interaction with my fans at the Western shows. There are all kinds, although a high percentage are older people with kids and grandkids who want their offspring to know the heroes of their youth. Since *Lawman* and *Laredo* are back on the air, we'll see if I acquire any new followers.

I do also get invited to TV collector shows where soap operas are still a big hit. For either genre, as long as I enjoy what I'm doing, I'll keep at it.

While these shows are a job of sorts, they're more of an excuse for us to go somewhere and have a good time. It's great to see the guys again. I relish the opportunity to visit with an east-coast guy like Will Hutchins at one of these shows; without these opportunities, I'm not sure when I'd ever get a chance to see Will or other east-coasters. And if you ever catch me at a show with longtime buddies Robert Fuller and William Smith, look out! Anything can happen then . . . and usually does.

I'm always amazed but happy that my long time fans still appreciate me for the work I've done. My fan website still exists at www.peterbrown.tv (Note that while it is approved by KK and me, we did not create the website.) It's full of news clippings, reviews, photos, magazine stories, and show synopses. There are also the mandatory opinions, hearsay, and gossip items just to keep things interesting. In a similar vein, I try to answer letters and e-mail as much as possible; thankfully my fans are always very respectful.

Speaking of my fans, there was one particular note sent to my website that, to this day, still warms me whenever I think about it. It was from a young lady we'll call "Jennifer." She wrote the following:

A few years ago, I was in a rather sad state of mind. I had been without a job for four months and was growing more and more depressed. One day, I found a book of celebrity addresses. So I figured, "Why not try it?"

The first letter I wrote was to Mr. Brown. Not once did I think he would actually respond to my letter. But exactly two weeks after it was mailed, I got a response. It completely surprised me. His response made me feel good about myself. So, I wrote a thank you letter to Mr. Brown. And again, he surprised me . . . He sent me a small picture with a note. And then two weeks after receiving Mr. Brown's first response, a computer company hired me.

Most people would say that I'm being silly, but I truly believe Mr. Brown saved my life. His response to my letters helped snap me out of my depression.

Now here I am at twenty-six and working for the local school district. My job may have changed but that feeling I had when I got Mr. Brown's response is still with me. And if by chance I were ever to meet Mr. Brown someday, I wouldn't know what to say besides "Thanks."

And to Jennifer I say, "Thank you!"

One of the great cowboy honors I received during my "retirement" occurred in 2000 when I was awarded, along with Dale Evans, Richard Farnsworth and Don Edwards, my own saddle on the Santa Clarita Valley's "Walk of Western Stars" in downtown Newhall, California. It was an incredible honor and was made even more special to me when they had my good friend Robert Fuller introduce me at the dinner ceremony.

The Walk goes back thirty-two years and includes such Western legends as John Wayne, Tom Mix, Gene Autry, and Roy Rogers. Pretty stellar company to be keeping for a mere "deputy," don't you think?

In 2002, I was honored to receive "The Golden Boot," the cowboy equivalent of the Oscar. This award was conceived of by that great character actor, Pat Buttram. He was most famous for first being Gene Autry's sidekick and later creating and inhabiting the memorable role of "Mr. Haney" on the very funny country television comedy *Green Acres*. Beginning in the early Eighties, the Golden Boot Award was established to honor actors and crew members who made significant contributions to westerns in both movies and TV. I had the incredibly good fortune to be inducted along with Peter Fonda, Stuart Whitman, longtime friend Robert Colbert, and *Lawman* executive producer William T. Orr among others. The gala, held in the International Ballroom at the Beverly Hilton Hotel, was a night I'll always remember.

After fifty-plus years in the business, it was so nice to receive recognition for my body of work. It's not why I did what I did, but still, it's always appreciated.

In 2007, a pair of honors were bestowed upon me. They both really made the day for this old cowboy. Kanab, Utah, is known as "Little Hollywood" for all the films, mostly westerns, that have been shot using that area's beautiful countryside as their giant outdoor set. The town's elders decided to honor the greats who had done movies in Kanab country by giving them a plaque on their own "Little Hollywood Walk of Fame." Honorees have included Ronald Reagan, Tom Mix, Glenn Ford, and Gabby Hayes. And as of 2007, you can add Peter Brown to that illustrious club. If you're ever in Kanab, keep an eye out for my plaque as you're touring the town.

Later that year, I was thrilled to be selected for a "Silver Spur" award. Established in 1997 by entertainment industry workers who were expected to have a clear understanding of the "cowboy mentality," these "Reel Cowboys," as they were called, had the desire to keep alive the wholesome good values and morals most often associated with and portrayed in western dramas. And in doing so, this "not-for-profit" organization was able to raise thousands of dollars each year for deserving charities. It was a real honor for me to be presented with this award, and as was becoming my usual method, it was presented to me again by KK's and my pal, Bruce Boxleitner.

As I'm writing this last chapter, I'm sitting outside my rented vacation condo not far from where I used to live. KK and I have come out here as a surprise getaway for her visiting father. As I lean back and face the ocean, so many memories from my life just come flooding back.

I'm not sure where to stop, but I better as we're heading out to a favorite Italian restaurant of ours, "The Bottle Inn," located just off the Strand in Hermosa Beach. A good friend of ours, Silvio Petoletti, owns it. We've been dining there for years. Silvio has a fantastic selection of wines from all over the world. And it is literally just twenty-five steps from the beach.

Watching the sunset on the patio at The Bottle Inn is a must for us; I've taken so many people there over the years including our close friends Rex and Robin Hardin. Rex is the great, great nephew of the legendary outlaw "John Wesley Hardin." How's that for irony . . . the nephew of a famous outlaw being best of friends with Deputy Johnny McKay?

Life is grand now. My wife KK and I enjoy doing so many things with each other, most of them outdoors when it's not too hot. Her boundless energy keeps me young. We love good food, wine, and champagne; and fortunately for me, she's a great cook. KK keeps an eye on our well-being by making sure we eat healthy.

We've traveled a lot in the years we've been together seeing such wonderful places as Paris, Costa Rica (three times), Australia (for one heckuva honeymoon), London, Italy, and Germany (several times to see KK's family). We're very excited about a trip to Ireland we've got planned in the spring of 2013. It just keeps getting better.

And of course there's my family. I thought having three wonderful kids was absolutely the best, at least, that is, until I became a grandfather. The three grandkids are the lights of my life. Granddaughter Stephanie went to college here in Phoenix, so I went through a second "proud father" phase when I attended most of her collegiate volleyball games. She's another one who really helps to keep me young. The two of us even dressed up and went to an Oscar party at our friends Rex and Robin's house and had the time of our lives. That incredible young lady is now in Germany playing professional volleyball for a year. I may have to go on some more long road trips to see her play.

I've also had real enjoyment with visits here in America from KK's mother while she was still with us and her father. This venerable, active gentleman from Germany keeps us on our toes. Although he speaks no English, and my German is limited to "Guten Morgen!" and "Bier," we get along famously and somehow we manage to make ourselves understood by each other.

A highlight of his last visit here was when KK and I took him to Los Angeles for a visit to the Playboy Mansion. Dad was thrilled. He even had his photo taken with Hef. I'm sure that while this part of my book is being written, he's at a bar somewhere in Deutschland showing the picture off to all his buddies.

Probably when I'm most at peace and contented nowadays is when I'm at home in the late afternoon just after KK has finished her work day. The knowledge of wine I picked up from good friend William Smith has stayed with me, so when KK comes downstairs from her office, I always have a glass of very good vintage vino already poured. It better be as KK has become quite the wine connoisseur over the years.

We sit out on our porch, sometimes joined by close friends, and just watch the lovely sunset over the desert vista. It's at times like these I can close my eyes and see the silhouette of a lone cowboy (who looks a lot like me) on horseback making his way into the evening sky.

Looking back on my life, I've had some real ups and downs, but all of it, the good and the bad, make up who I am today. I wouldn't change a minute of it for anything. And I plan on making more great memories for years to come. I've got a lot of living left to do.

In going back through all the memorabilia and scrapbooks that make up a small part of my life (Yes, I actually had to research my own life), I came across an interview I did just after my first marriage. I think it was *TV Guide*. The interviewer had posed a lot of questions. She finished up by asking me what I wanted to accomplish in the rest of my life. Now remember that this was over fifty years ago.

I recall being stuck at first, but after a moment of thought, it all became clear to me, almost as if I could see directly into my future.

"My goals in life are simple," I said. "They're threefold actually: one, to have a loving and committed relationship with the woman of my dreams; two, to have a big family with children and someday grandchildren who are all happy, healthy, and (eventually) wise; and three . . . "

I winked at the interviewer.

". . . to be able to act as well as Sidney Poitier."

In retrospect, I'm married to the woman of my dreams, so check that one off; I've got three great kids and three of the world's best grandkids, all thriving and doing well, so check that one off the goals' list as well; and as far as Sidney . . .

Well, two out of three ain't bad.

Peter Brown's Filmography and Television Credits

1956   RECRUITING FOR THE U.S. ARMY (television commercial)

1957   MATINEE THEATRE "The Lonely Look" (television series)
MATINEE THEATRE "Madam Ada" (television series)
MATINEE THEATRE "The Brat's House" (television series)
MATINEE THEATRE "The Remarkable Mr. Jerome" (television series)
SAYONARA (uncredited)
DARBY'S RANGERS
COLT .45 "The Peacemaker" (television series)
COLT .45 "Young Gun" (television series)
MAVERICK "Point Blank" (television series)
MAVERICK "Stage West" (television series)
CHEYENNE "Top Hand" (television series)

1958   GATEWAYS TO THE MIND (television science documentary)
MARJORIE MORNINGSTAR (uncredited)
VIOLENT ROAD (uncredited)
NO TIME FOR SERGEANTS (uncredited)
ONIONHEAD
SUGARFOOT "Hideout" (television series)
CHEYENNE "Renegades" (television series)
CHEYENNE "Ghost of the Cimarron" (television series)
LAWMAN (television series, 4 years)
THE PAT BOONE CHEVY SHOWROOM (television series)

1959   WESTBOUND (uncredited)
THE YOUNG PHILADELPHIANS (uncredited)
SUGARFOOT "The Trial of the Canary Kid" (television series)

1960   MAVERICK "Hadley's Hunters" (television series)

1961   HERE'S HOLLYWOOD (television series)

1962   FREEDOM AND YOU (aka RED NIGHTMARE)
(film short for U.S. Defense Department)
MERRILL'S MARAUDERS
HAWAIIAN EYE "Lalama Lady" (television series)
CHEYENNE "Pocketful of Stars" (television series)
77 SUNSET STRIP "The Gang's All Here" (television series)
77 SUNSET STRIP "Wolf, Cried the Blonde" (television series)

1963   THE ALFRED HITCHCOCK HOUR "Forecast: Low Clouds and Coastal Fog" (television series)
THE ALFRED HITCHCOCK HOUR "Death of a Cop" (television series)
THE GALLANT MEN "The Bridge" (television series)
WAGON TRAIN "The Adam MacKenzie Story" (television series)
SUMMER MAGIC
REDIGO "The Blooded Bull" (television series)

1964   A TIGER WALKS RIDE THE WILD SURF
KITTEN WITH A WHIP
WAGON TRAIN "The Geneva Balfour Story" (television series)
WAGON TRAIN "Those Who Stay Behind" (television series)
KRAFT SUSPENSE THEATRE "The Action of the Tiger" (television series)
KRAFT SUSPENSE THEATRE "One Tiger to a Hill" (television series)
THE VIRGINIAN "Return a Stranger" (television series)
THE VIRGINIAN "We've Lost a Train" (television series)

1965   LAREDO (television series, 2 years)
THE INVISIBLE CIRCLE (motorcycle safety education film)

1967   THE DANNY THOMAS HOUR "The Enemy" (television series)
THE VIRGINIAN "A Small Taste of Justice" (television series)

1968   THREE GUNS FOR TEXAS
YOUR ALL-AMERICAN COLLEGE SHOW (television series)

1969   THE BEST YEARS (television movie)
MOD SQUAD "The Debt" (television series)

1970   HUNTERS ARE FOR KILLING (television movie)
EAGLES ATTACK AT DAWN
THE MOST DEADLY GAME "War Games" (television series)

1971   DAYS OF OUR LIVES (television series, 8 years)
MY THREE SONS "The Love God" (television series)
DAN AUGUST "The Manufactured Man" (television series)
MISSION: IMPOSSIBLE "Blind" (television series)
CHROME AND HOT LEATHER
O'HARA, U.S. TREASURY "Operation: Spread" (television series)

1972   PIRANHA, PIRANHA
MEDICAL CENTER "Deadlock" (television series)
THE BOB NEWHART SHOW "Tennis, Emily?" (television series)

1973   GENTLE SAVAGE (executive producer)
THE MAGICIAN "The Vanishing Lady" (television series)

1974   FOXY BROWN
       MEMORY OF US
       ACT OF VIOLENCE (aka RAPE SQUAD)
       POLICE STORY "The Gamble" (television series)
       POLICE STORY "Love, Mabel" (television series)

1975   CELEBRITY BOWLING (television series)
       SUNBURST
       MARCUS WELBY, M.D. "The Covenant" (television series)
       MATT HELM "Dead Men Talk" (television series)
       MATT HELM "Murder on Ice" (television series)
       POLICE WOMAN "Above and Beyond" (television series)

1977   THE STREETS OF SAN FRANCISCO "One Last Trick" (television
       series)
       QUINCY, M.E. "Main Man" (television series)

1978   CHARLIE'S ANGELS "Angels Ahoy" (television series)
       VEGA$ "The Pageant" (television series)
       THE EDDIE CAPRA MYSTERIES "Breakout to Murder" (television series)
       FLYING HIGH "Brides and Grooms" (television series)

1979   SALVAGE 1 "Salvage" (television series)
       WHEN THE WEST WAS FUN (television special)
       PROJECT U.F.O. "The Atlantic Queen Incident" (television series)
       CALIFORNIA FEVER "Beach Wars" (television series)

1980   THE DUKES OF HAZZARD "Officer Daisy Duke" (television series)
       TOP OF THE HILL (television movie)
       THE GIRL, THE GOLD WATCH AND EVERYTHING (television movie)

1981   YOUNG AND THE RESTLESS (television series, 2 years)
       FANTASY ISLAND "The Artist and the Lady" (television series)
       THE MISADVENTURES OF SHERIFF LOBO "Airsick" (television series)

1982   DALLAS "Denial" (television series)
       THE CONCRETE JUNGLE
       MAGNUM, P.I. "Heal Thyself" (television series)
       CAR CARE CENTRAL (television series, 1 year)

1983   TEENAGE TEASE (aka Bleep)
       HART TO HART "As the Hart Turns" (television series)
       T.J. HOOKER "Carnal Express" (television series)
       T.J. HOOKER "Chinatown" (television series)
       MANIMAL "High Stakes" (television series)
       LOVING (television series, 2 years)

1984 SIMON AND SIMON "The Dillinger Print" (television series)
    CALENDAR GIRL MURDERS (television movie)
    WHIZ KIDS "Father's Day" (television series)
    COVER UP "Pilot" (television series)
    THE FALL GUY "San Francisco Caper" (television series)
    RIPTIDE "Peter Pan is Alive and Well" (television series)

1985 CRAZY LIKE A FOX "Till Death Do Us Part" (television series)
    KNIGHT RIDER "knight Behind Bars" (television series)

1986 ONE LIFE TO LIVE (television series, 2 years)
    SIMON AND SIMON "Mobile Home of the Brave" (television series)
    AIRWOLF "Little Wolf" (television series)
    THE AURORA ENCOUNTER
    THE A-TEAM "The Theory of Revolution" (television series)
    THE MESSENGER

1988 OHARA "Last Year's Model" (television series)
    AARON'S WAY "New Patterns" (television series)
    1ST & TEN: THE CHAMPIONSHIP "Caught in the Draft"
    (television series)

1989 YOUNG AND THE RESTLESS (television series, 2 years)
    HUNTER "Partners" (television series)
    GENERATIONS (television series)

1990 DEMONSTONE
    BAYWATCH "Shark Derby" (television series)

1991 BOLD AND THE BEAUTIFUL (television series, 2 years)

1992 WINGS "Noses Off" (television series)

1994 ONE WEST WAIKIKI "Along Came a Spider" (television series)

1995 FISTS OF IRON

1997 ASYLUM

1999 WASTELAND JUSTICE

2000 JAG "Real Deal Seal" (television series)

2004 HOLLYWOOD, IT'S A DOG LIFE (aka BIG CHUCK, LITTLE CHUCK)
    Y.M.I.

2005 THREE BAD MEN HELL TO PAY

About Alexx Stuart

Scottsdale playwright Alexx Stuart has been called "the king of humorous stage plays about sports." That may be because five of his eleven plays are about baseball, football, golf, or softball. He's also written a sports novel, a screenplay, and several very angry "Letters to the Editor."

A graduate of both Carleton College and the Brown Institute of Broadcasting, Stuart was a sports columnist for five years in Minnesota. In Arizona, he won the prestigious "Arizona Series" award for his first play, *Buzzard Ball*. He was also the head writer for the Phoenix-based sketch comedy group, "The Early Bird Special."

Alexx is a member of the Dramatists Guild and the Minnesota Softball Hall of Fame. He and wife Diedre Kaye owned their own theater production company from 2004-2011.

Working on his first biography, Alexx was inspired by his wife's teenage recollection of having Peter's poster on her bedroom wall. Amazingly, Diedre was able to make it to every interview session Alexx had with Peter.

Index

CPSIA information can be obtained at www.ICGtesting.com
Printed in the USA
LVOW07s0859170713

343295LV00008B/282/P